ENTERING THE KINGDOM

Michael Jones

ENTERING THE KINGDOM

KNOWING THE DETAILS OF A CHRISTIAN'S SALVATION

MICHAEL JONES

Entering the Kingdom by Michael Jones
Copyright © 2021 by Michael Jones
All Rights Reserved.
ISBN: 978-1-59755-663-7

Published by: ADVANTAGE BOOKS™   www.advbookstore.com

This book and parts thereof may not be reproduced in any form, stored in a retrieval system or transmitted in any form by any means (electronic, mechanical, photocopy, recording or otherwise) without prior written permission of the author, except as provided by United States of America copyright law.

Unless otherwise indicated, Scripture quotations are taken from THE HOLY BIBLE, ENGLISH STANDARD VERSION®(ESV) Copyright© 2001 by Crossway, a publishing ministry of Good News Publishers. Used by permission.

Scripture quotations marked (NAB) are taken from the NEW AMERICAN BIBLE© 2010, 1991, 1986, 1970 Confraternity of Christian Doctrine, Washington, D.C. and are used by permission of the copyright owner. All Rights Reserved. No part of the New American Bible may be reproduced in any form without permission in writing from the copyright owner.

Library of Congress Catalog Number: 2022930429

Names:	Jones, Michael, Author
Title:	Entering the Kingdom: Knowing every detail about a Christians Salvation / Michael Jones
Description	Advantage Books, 2022
Identifiers:	ISBN (print): 9781597556637, (mobi, epub): 9781597556774
Subjects:	Christian Life: Inspirational

First Printing June 2022
22 23 24 25 26 27   10 9 8 7 6 5 4 3 2 1

Table of Contents

INTRODUCTION 7

1: WHO GOD IS AND WHY HE MADE US 9

2: HOW GOD MADE US AND DESIGNED US 21

3: WHAT SIN IS AND HOW IT AFFECTS US 31

4: WHY GOD LIMITS OUR LIVES AND WE DIE 43

5: WHY GOD LIMITS OUR KNOWLEDGE OF HIM 53

6: WHY GOD LIMITS OUR ABILITY TO GLORIFY HIM 67

7: WHO JESUS WOULD BE AND WHAT HE WOULD ESTABLISH 79

8: HOW JESUS CAME TO ESTABLISH HIS KINGDOM 93

9: THE MINISTRY OF JESUS AND WHAT HE DID FOR US 107

10: WHAT JESUS' MINISTRY PROVIDED FOR US 121

11: JESUS PERFORMED HIS MINISTRY THROUGH POSITIONS 133

12: WHAT GOD DID TO BRING US TO JESUS AND INTO HIS KINGDOM 143

13: WHO THE HOLY SPIRIT IS AND HOW HE MADE US RIGHTEOUS 155

14: WHAT THE HOLY SPIRIT DID AFTER HE MADE US RIGHTEOUS 165

15: HOW CHRIST'S RIGHTEOUSNESS CAUSES US TO GLORIFY GOD 179

CONCLUSION 191

Michael Jones

Introduction

We occasionally get into conversations with non-Christians about our salvation. These conversations are not usually planned. We are talking to a particular non-Christian about this or that and before we realize it, we are talking religion. For us as Christians, talking religion with non-Christians means talking about Jesus and salvation. When we talk about salvation, non-Christians are not usually shy. They often ask us pointed questions. They may ask us to explain the Trinity and how God can exist as a man. They may ask us to explain the connection between Jesus' death hundreds of years ago and their lives right now. After they ask questions such as these, they will often pause and be charitable so that we can think for a second and give them a response. Often, however, we may not know exactly how to respond. All we end up doing is answering them in such a way as to save face. Our answers are usually far from being helpful and beneficial to them. As a result, we come to the stark realization that we do not know as much as we thought we did about our salvation.

I wrote this book for Christians who want to obtain a thorough understanding of their own salvation. Many of us have read enough books on this subject that when we read another one, we can almost finish the author's sentence. This book is not one of those. This book does more than just give a brief sketch of our salvation, it explains our salvation in detail. It explains logically and chronologically the what, where, when, how, and why of our salvation.

In writing this book, I approached the subject of our salvation differently than we may be used to hearing. Sometimes when we read about some detail of our salvation, it comes from the perspective of us; what happened to us or what we got. There is no shortage of people who will explain what we get from being saved. Our salvation, however, is not about what we get. Our salvation is about God. God saved us for a specific purpose, and this purpose pertains to him, not us. God created us to glorify him. In order for us to glorify God, God made us righteous, saved us out of the sinful world, and placed us into his kingdom where he rules us. We exist in God's kingdom to glorify him.

Some Christians may consider the views within this book to be controversial. These views may go against those they have learned and wrestled with for years. However, all the views within this book are based on a correct interpretation of Scripture. At the end of the day, if Christians have to choose between views that are controversial and views that are scripturally sound, they will usually take the latter. They know that when it comes to understanding every detail about their salvation, the Scriptures can and will teach them. My hope is that this book will spiritually enrich those who read it and give them a refreshed understanding of their salvation.

Chapter 1

Who God Is and Why He Made Us

A man walked into a coworker's office one day and sat down. The man was a non-Christian, and he went to his coworker's office because he knew his coworker was a Christian. The non-Christian sat there for a few moments while the Christian continued working. Eventually, the non-Christian looked at the Christian and asked him the mother of all questions. He asked him what the meaning of life was. He could have asked him who Cain had married, or how Noah had gotten all the animals on the Ark, but he did not. He asked him one of more serious questions that any of us ask. He asked him about our purpose for existing.

At various times in our lives, we each have thought about why we exist. We have also thought about whether it would matter to anyone if we did not. We have thought about things such as these because deep within each of us we know that we exist for a purpose. We know that nothing exists that does not also have a purpose for existing. There is no such thing as a random entity that happened to come into existence without a purpose. The fact is, we do exist for a purpose. The purpose for which we exist is directly related to who God is. This is the key to understanding who we are. We are who we are because of who God is.

Who God Is

When we think about who are God is, it is important for us to realize that our God is the true God, and he is the only God who actually exists. There are no other gods except our God. To phrase this in theological terms, he is the only true objective God. When we seek to understand our purpose, it is the true objective God who has given it to us. Non-Christians, however, may indeed believe in false gods, but these gods do not actually exist, and they certainly have not given us our purpose. False gods only exist within the minds of non-Christians. To also phrase this in theological terms, all false gods are subjective gods because they do not actually exist in reality. They only exist in a non-Christian's mind. 1 Corinthians 8:4 says, "We know that 'an idol has no real existence,' and that 'there is no God but [the only] one.'"

Non-Christians believe in false gods because they have a basic idea in their minds that some kind of god or divine being exists. They believe in gods such as Allah as the Islamic god, Thor as a Pagan god, or Shiva as a Hindu god. 1 Corinthians 8:5-6 says, "For although there may be so-called gods in heaven or on earth -- as indeed there are many 'gods' and many 'lords.'" If a particular non-Christian believes that only one false god exists, and he follows its religion, he follows a monotheistic religion. If a non-Christian believes several false gods exists, even if he only worships one of them, and he follows its religion, he follows a polytheistic religion. If a non-Christian believes that his false god is collectively everything in the creation, and he follows its religion, he follows a pantheistic religion. Regardless of what kind of gods non-Christians follow, their gods do not actually exist. The Scriptures affirm to us in three ways that other gods do not exist, and our God is the only one who does.

First, the Scriptures indicate that God is the only God by directly explaining that other gods do not actually exist. The Scriptures do this because stating this fact directly is the most basic way to explain that God exists. An example of this occurs in Acts 17:23-29. In this passage, the Apostle Paul explained that when he arrived in Athens, he walked through the city and examined the objects that the Athenians had made and worshipped. Paul noticed an altar with an inscription, "To an unknown god," signifying to him that the Athenians knew they were children of some kind of god or divine being, but they did not know him. Paul tells the Athenians in Acts 17:29, "We ought not to think that the divine being is like gold or silver or stone, an image formed by the art and imagination of man." Paul also told them directly that the one true God is the only one who actually exists.

The Scriptures indicate in a second way that God is the only one by using the phrase "God is one" or "The Lord is one." This phrase originally occurred in Deuteronomy 6:4 which says, "The Lord is one." The English word "one" in this verse is based on the Hebrew word *echad*. A biblical translator can translate *echad* with a numerical nuance meaning "one" as opposed to "two" or "three." However, a biblical translator can also translate *echad* with an exclusive nuance meaning "only one." The biblical translators of many Bible versions often used the word "one" with the numerical nuance.[1] This, however, does not accurately denote the true meaning. The accurate translation is

---

[1] A person's misunderstanding of the word "one" in this context has been a major factor in the theological view called "Modalism."

"only one" with the exclusive nuance. Deuteronomy 6:4 should read "the Lord is the only one."

We can see that this is accurate by analyzing other passages such as Mark 12:32. Mark 12:32 paraphrases Deuteronomy 6:4, and then explains what it means when it says, "He is one, and there is no other besides him." The first phrase is the paraphrase from Deuteronomy 6:4. The second phrase is the explanation, and shows that the word "one" should be translated "only one" when used in the phrase "God is one." God is the only God, and when we understand how the Scriptures use language, this becomes clear.

The Scriptures indicate in a third way that God is the only one by using the phrases the "alpha and the omega," the "first and the last," or the "beginning and the end." Revelation 22:13 says, "I am the Alpha and the Omega, the first and last, the beginning and the end." These three phrases explain God existed before he created the world and will exist after the world passes away. As such, all the false gods that supposedly existed in between are not real. We can see this repeatedly in the book of Isaiah. Isaiah desired to show Israel that the false gods they worshipped were not gods. In doing so, he called the true God the first God and the last God. Isaiah 44:6 says, "I am the first and I am the last; besides me there is no god."

Our God is the one true objective God, and his purpose for us is objectively true. This is one of things that distinguishes us from non-Christians. Non-Christians can give themselves whatever purpose they want because their gods only exist in their minds. For us, however, the true God gave us a definitive purpose. God's purpose for us is directly related to who he is. Specifically, the true God's purpose for us is directly related to his qualities. Any entity that exists has qualities. The entity and its qualities are inseparable. God as an entity has qualities, and they are intrinsic to who he is. God has always existed with his qualities, and he always will. God's purpose for us then is directly related to his qualities.

God Is Spirit

God's basic quality is that he exists as a spirit in form. John 4:24 says, "God is spirit." A spirit will have spiritual characteristics such as intellect, will, and emotion. As such, God as spirit has an intellect. He can reason and think. He also has a will. He can decide to do and say things. He also has emotions. He can be happy and angry. God has intellect, will, and emotions because he is spirit. As spirit, God exists in three spiritual forms. No other spiritual being exists in three spiritual forms except God.

When we first hear this, we may assume that there are three different Gods, but this is not the case. When we refer to God as existing in three different spiritual forms or persons, we are referring to his internal constitution.

God's Constitution

God's constitution refers to his collective make-up. We refer to many things using their collective make-up. For example, we may say that New York City is made up of five boroughs. Each borough is part of New York City. This is its collective make-up. We may say that a loaf of sliced bread is made up of 25 slices. Each slice is part of the loaf. This is its collective make-up. Similarly, God exists in three distinct spiritual forms. This is his collective make-up. The names of these three spiritual forms are God the Father, Jesus the Son, and the Holy Spirit. The Scriptures mention the three spiritual forms of God in many different places. Occasionally, however, they go further and mention each of them in the same passage. One such passage is Matthew 28:19. In this passage, Jesus tells his disciples to spiritually baptize people of all nations in the name of the Father, the Son, and the Holy Spirit. Jesus' reference to these three distinct spiritual forms shows that God exists with this type of constitution.

All Three Spiritual Forms of God Are Divine

The very essence or substance of each spiritual form is wholly divine. We may be a little prone to think that God the Father is more divine than Jesus the Son or the Holy Spirit. It is not unreasonable for us to think this because he is the Father. This, however, is not the case. It is true that God the Father is higher than Jesus the Son and the Holy Spirit in *position*. He can tell Jesus and the Holy Spirit what to speak, and he can send them to say and do certain things. However, God the Father, Jesus, and the Holy Spirit are all equal as it pertains to their *essence*. Jesus and the Holy Spirit are no less divine than God the Father.

This is not all there is. The three distinct spiritual forms of God all exist simultaneously with each other and always have. This means God did not start off as the Father, then change into the Son, and change again into the Holy Spirit.[2] This also means that the names God the Father, Jesus the Son, and the Holy Spirit are not simply three different names for the same spiritual form. Rather, God the Father, Jesus the Son, and the Holy Spirit have eternally existed together as three distinct spiritual forms.

---

[2] This view is called Modalism.

Entering the Kingdom

We can see this in the Scriptures with Jesus himself. In Matthew 3:16-17, we read about Jesus' baptism. When Jesus was baptized, God the Father, and the Holy Spirit were in Heaven, while Jesus was on the earth. When Jesus came up out of the water, the Holy Spirit descended from Heaven and came upon him. Then the voice of God the Father came from Heaven and said, "This is my beloved Son, with whom I am well pleased." God the Father was in Heaven, Jesus the Son was on Earth, and the Holy Spirit went from the former to the latter thereby showing that the three spiritual forms of God exist simultaneously with each other.

God constitutes three distinct spiritual forms because of how each spiritual form works with each other to ultimately work in our lives. Each spiritual form performs different work in our lives as it pertains to giving us our purpose of glorifying God and helping us fulfill it. This means God does not just happen to be made up of three spiritual forms. God is specifically made-up of three spiritual forms because he exists with this type of constitution to enable us to glorify him.[3] God exists the way he is, so he could work the way he does, to cause us to live the way he wants.

The nature of God's constitution can be confusing even for the most mature Christians. For some of us, understanding how God can exist in three forms may still be a little unclear. The analogy of H2O may clear up some confusion. H2O is a molecular compound consisting of two hydrogen and one oxygen atoms. This compound can exist in three distinct physical forms, specifically solid, liquid, and gas. Each of these have the corresponding names, ice, water, and vapor. All three of these physical *forms* have the same H2O *essence,* and they always will. All three of these distinct physical forms with the same essence also exist simultaneously with each other. If we place a glass of ice water on a picnic table on a sunny day, the sun will cause evaporation though we may not see it. Ice, water, and vapor will all be simultaneously present in that glass. Likewise, God exists in three distinct spiritual forms. They are each fully divine and exist simultaneously with each.

We may not think we would ever need to explain God's constitution to someone, but there may be occasions when we will need to. If we are explaining who Jesus is in relation to God, we may need to explain his divinity, and therefore, God's constitution. If we are explaining certain passages of Scripture, we may need to explain God's constitution. When we do, however, we may not always want to explain all the various

---

[3] If the true God is made-up of three distinct spiritual forms for the specific purpose of causing us to live righteously, then any god who is not made-up of three distinct spiritual forms is a false god.

facets of God's constitution as this may be very time consuming. Instead, as we explain God's constitution, we may simply use the term "Trinity."

The Trinity

We as Christians use the word trinity to explain God's constitution because it is a combination of the words "tri" and "unity." We say that God exists as a trinity because he exists as three distinct spiritual forms which are united. We also use the corresponding phrase, "The three persons of the trinity." The concept of person or member means an individual as distinct from the group. God is a trinity because he constitutes three distinct spiritual forms, persons, or members. Some of us realize that the word trinity is not in the Scriptures, and this may initially cause a little uneasiness among us. However, we can be rest assured, it is alright for us to use it. We as Christians came up with this term to describe God's constitution for purposes of brevity instead of having to elaborate on the concept in detail. Instead of having to explain that God exists in three spiritual forms, that they are all divine, and that they exist simultaneously with each other, we simply use the term trinity.

It is not uncommon for us in other areas of our lives to use a single word or phrase to describe a complex concept. For example, in basketball there are five ways to achieve merit; field goals, assists, steals, rebounds, and blocked shots. The college and professional basketball rulebooks mention all of these ways. If a player gets ten or more in any three of these categories, we refer to this concept with the simple term "triple double." Though the rulebooks mention the various ways to achieve merit, they do not mention the term "triple double." We simply came up with this term for brevity sake. The same thing is true with our use of the term trinity. The Scriptures explain the *concept* of the trinity even though they do not use the *term*. We simply use the term for brevity sake.

Some of the things pertaining to God are light and easy. We know God exists as spirit. Most of us know this. However, other things are deep and difficult. God exists in three distinct spiritual forms who exist simultaneous with each other. Some of us may not completely understand this. One thing we can be sure of and understand without much difficulty is that our God has a name.

The One God Is Named Yahweh

God's name is Yahweh. We got our names by our parents when we were born, but our names may not have any relevance to who we are. This is not true with God. God's name has a specific meaning. It pertains specifically to who he is and who we are.

The first reference to God in the Scriptures occurs in Genesis 1:1. In this verse, the writer of Genesis refers to God using the Hebrew word *Elohim*. Elohim is the pluralized form of the Hebrew word *El*, which means deity. The word Elohim, however, is a position, not a name.[4] God's name was and is Yahweh. God gave himself his own name and began telling his people to call him his name when he established Israel as a nation. Exodus 3:13-15 says, "Then Moses said to God, 'If I come to the people of Israel and say to them, "The God of your fathers has sent me to you," and they ask me, "What is his name?" what shall I say to them?' God said to Moses, 'I AM [*ehyeh*] WHO I AM [*ehyeh*].' And he said, 'Say this to the people of Israel: "I AM [*ehyeh*] has sent me to you."' God also said to Moses, 'Say this to the people of Israel: "The Lord [*yhweh*], the God of your Fathers."'"

If we look closely at the Hebrew in these verses, we may see that in verse 14, God calls himself "I am," but in verse 15 he calls himself "Yahweh." There is a logical explanation to this variation. It shows that the name Yahweh is a variant of the phrase "I am." The phrase "I am" means "I exist." However, when God calls himself the "I am," it means more than just that he exists. There are many things that exist. We exist, and the things we see around us exist. However, we do not call ourselves "I am" just because we exist. Neither does God. God refers to himself as "I am" and the variant "Yahweh" because he has established all that there is. Yahweh means "I am," but its nuance means "Establisher." Everything exists and has come into being because God decreed that it would. The source of all things is God because he is Yahweh, the "I am," or the Establisher. He established everything including us so we would glorify him. God's name is directly related to us and the purpose for our existence.

As we read the Scriptures, we may have noticed one important detail that is common among many of the major translations. They do not use the Hebrew name Yahweh. Instead, they use the English name Lord. Our thoughts about this may be that the translators are incorrect or just unsure of what to call God, but neither is the case. The reason most translations use the English name Lord is fairly simple. When the Old

---

[4] This is similar to how we refer to our earthly fathers. We may call them "Dad" which is a title, not a name.

Testament writers wrote about the true God, they used the Hebrew name Yahweh which means "establisher." When the New Testament writers wrote about Yahweh, they used the Greek name k*upios*, which also means "establisher." Then when English translators wanted to convey the meaning of "establisher" they chose the English name "Lord." As such, many translations use the name Lord in the Old Testament as a translation of Yahweh, and they use Lord in the New Testament as a translation of kupios. Our God, the Lord, established us and made us for the purpose of glorifying him. Our glorifying God, however, is not based on our living however we feel like. We glorify God by displaying his objective qualities which he gave to us to display.

The Qualities of Our God

Everything has qualities, and when we speak of anything, we speak of its qualities. When a mother speaks of her son, she describes his qualities. She may say that he is kind, generous, flexible, and insightful. We describe all kinds of people with qualities, and we do the same with God. Broadly speaking, God's qualities are life, knowledge, power, and righteousness. God has more qualities than these, but most of his qualities fall under these four broad categories. God's qualities are inherent to who he is, meaning he is these qualities and does not possess them. God does not possess his qualities because if something possesses a quality, it can exist without that quality. God, however, does not exist without his qualities. If we explain God, but add or subtract from his qualities, we are not discussing the essence of the true God, but rather the essence of a man-made god. When we speak of God's qualities, we can speak of them both qualitatively and quantitatively.

God Is Perfect

Qualitatively speaking, God's qualities of life, knowledge, power, and righteousness are perfect. Something is perfect if it does not have any flaws in it. At the elementary level, a flaw in an object is the absence of something necessary or the presence of something unnecessary for that object to be perfect according to its intended design. For example, if a bridge contains something unnecessary such as extra rails or it lacks something necessary such as missing rails, it has a flaw. The bridge is not perfect according to its intended design. This is why the concept of perfection is the same as the concept of completeness. God is perfect or complete because there are no flaws in his qualities. God is called perfect in passages such as Matthew 5:48 which says, "As your heavenly Father is perfect."

Because God's qualities are perfect, he will never change, and would never have to. Each time anything changes at the substantive level, it loses part of its qualities, gains part of its qualities, or both. As this applies to God, he will never gain qualities and evolve into anything more advanced, nor will God lose qualities and deteriorate into decrepitude. Rather, God will remain unchanged in his qualities throughout all eternity. As such, we refer to God as being unchangeable or immutable. The Scriptures speak about God's unchanging nature in Malachi 3:1-6. In this passage, God had prophesied over a period of several hundred years that he would destroy Israel because of their sin and his holiness. However, he would save a remnant of them through the Lord who will come to make them holy. God then says in verse 6, "For I the Lord do not change." God said this because he would save them as he promised. God's unchanging nature gave Israel hope and comfort knowing that God would do as he promised.

As we read the Scriptures, however, we may have noticed that they occasionally speak of God changing. Some passages seem to indicate God does change, while others indicate that he does not. For example, Amos 7:6 says, "The Lord relented concerning this." The word relent has the connotation of changing one's mind or heart. However, James 1:17 says, "The Father of lights, with whom there is no variation or shadow due to change." This may cause us to wonder whether or not God changes.

We can resolve this apparent contradiction by understanding that in cases where the Scriptures teach that God changes, they are not referring to a change in God's qualities. They are referring to a change in how God deals with us. God changes how he deals with us based on the changes we make in how we live, even when God is the one who directs those changes to take place. For example, as God deals with us who are sinful, God will change the way he acts toward us as we repent of our sin or fluctuate in our actions, even when God is cause of those fluctuations.

We see this in the analogy of a father and son. A father may give his son the task of taking out the garbage. He may do this to teach him responsibility. The father does not change his expectations for the son, and the son always has to take the garbage out. On occasion, however, the son may forget to do it. The father may tell the son that because he has not taken out the trash, he cannot go out and play. However, if the son quickly takes out the trash, the father may change his mind and let the son go out and play. In this situation, the father treated the son fairly and rightly, but he treated him differently as the son changed in how he obeyed, even when the father was the cause of his obedience. God is the same way. God's qualities do not change. He is perfect and he always does the right thing. However, he may work differently in our lives as we interact with him and change how we live, even when he causes us to.

Sometimes it may be difficult for us to imagine God being perfect with respect to life or knowledge or power because we are limited in these qualities ourselves. God, however, is perfect, and he will never do anything inappropriate or make a mistake. Even when we do not understand why God is working in our lives in a certain way, God will never work in the wrong way, and have to undo it. We may be tempted to think God is wrong, and that he may not be fully aware of what he is doing especially when we are not happy with our lives. However, God knows exactly what he is doing all the time and in all circumstances. God's qualities and the works which come from them are perfect.

In addition to our understanding God's qualities in a qualitative way, we can also understand God's qualities in a quantitative way.

God Is Infinite

Quantitatively speaking, God's qualities of life, knowledge, power, and righteousness are infinite. Something is infinite if it is not limited by anything. This is easy to say, but hard to see. The concept of infinity does not actually exist in the physical world. There is no physical object anywhere in the universe that is infinite. We cannot even find the concept of infinity in the physical universe to show that it exists or prove that it is true. However, we can attribute infinity to God because he is not part of the physical universe, but rather the source of it. We attribute infinity to God because his qualities are indeed infinite. They are not limited to the extent God chooses to express them as he works in the world in accordance with his will.

When we talk about God's infinite nature, we often do so only with respect to time and space, and refer to him as eternal and omnipresent, respectively. This is certainly true, but we can also talk about God as being infinite with respect to his four broad qualities. We can say that God is not limited in life so he is omnificent. We can say that God is not limited in knowledge so he is omniscient. We can say that God is not limited in power so he is omnipotent. We can say that God is not limited in righteousness so he is immaculate. We can apply the concept of infinity to all four of God's qualities and describe him.

God Works in Us as an Extension of His Qualities

All of God's perfect and infinite qualities are in harmony with each other. There is no disharmony or disunity within God as it pertains to his qualities. Furthermore, God exercises his harmonious qualities through his works in the world. God will never perform any work in the world that is not a direct extension of his perfect and infinite qualities. God's works are also in harmony with each other because they come from his qualities, which are harmony. God does not perform any work inconsistent with another work, such as change history or sin because this would indicate a disharmony, not only in his works, but also in his qualities.

We can understand the harmony between God's works through the analogy of a general contractor. A general contractor builds houses, but he himself does not do the work. He uses different subcontractors to do the work for him such as carpenters, plumbers, and electricians. All the various subcontractors work in harmony with the general contractor who has established the plans for the house. Because of this, they also work in harmony with each other, and construct the house exactly the way the general contractor wants.

God's inherent qualities are perfect and infinite, and each of his qualities are in harmony with the others. This means for us that God will always work in our lives in such a way that corresponds to his perfect and infinite qualities of life, knowledge, power, and righteousness. We may not understand how he does this, but he does because he is perfect and infinite

God's Qualities Cause Him to Have Glory

The one true God has perfect and infinite qualities, and he is the only one who does. God, with these perfect and infinite qualities, is absolutely magnificent. Our minds and hearts cannot comprehend the majesty of the one true God. In the midst of absolutely nothing, he spoke…and the beauty of the sky and the details of our bodies ultimately came into existence. God knows perfectly the deepest part of the ocean and the most remote corner of space. The one true God exists in a state of absolute excellence and greatness, and this causes him to have immense glory. 1 Chronicles 29:11 says, "Yours, O Lord, is the greatness and the power and the glory and the victory and the majesty." The Hebrew word for glory is *kabode*, and Greek word is *doxa*. Each of these words mean a display of excellence or richness. Because God's qualities are both perfect and infinite, he has the highest amount of glory. We cannot compare or measure the amount of glory of the one true God. We cannot even describe with words the level of glory of the one true God. This is where we come in, and humbly so.

God Reflects His Glory through Us

God's purpose for making us is to reflect his glory. God made us and brought each of us into existence so that we would reflect his glory. Prior to God's making us and the universe for us, nothing reflected God's glory because nothing existed. God, however, in his well-deserved and most judicial decision created us to reflect him. We exist to show and reveal the majesty of the one true God. Our purpose in doing this is the highest purpose of any entity anywhere within the creation. We exist for God and to reveal his glory. God himself has glory because he has the qualities of life, knowledge, and power and righteousness perfectly and infinitely. God enables us to reflect his glory by transferring these qualities to us to a certain degree so that we have glory. 2 Corinthians 3:5 says, "Not that we are adequate in ourselves to consider anything as coming from ourselves, but our adequacy is from God." When we display God's qualities in our lives, we reflect him and glorify him.

We see this concept through the analogy of a painter. If a painter has exceptional knowledge, skills, and ability, he is an exceptional painter in his essential nature. His nature as an exceptional painter causes him to have glory. However, no one sees his glory until he creates a painting. When he does, the painting is a beautiful masterpiece. Everything about the colors, symmetry, and mood of the painting is very well done. The painting in its essential nature is of high quality and has glory. When a person sees the painting, he instantly realizes that the old adage that beauty is in the eye of the beholder is product of a fool's wisdom.

Rather, he sees that the essential nature of the painting is objectively beautiful, and it has glory. The glory of the painting reflects back on the painter and gives him glory. In a similar way, God gave us the qualities of life, knowledge, power, and righteousness. God made us to have these qualities so we would reflect him and glorify him as the one true God. God made us to be a work of art of high quality so we would reflect him as our creator and God. This is God's purpose for making us.

Chapter 2

How God Made Us and Designed Us

A hardware store sells different types of hammers. It sells claw hammers, ball-peen hammers, rubber mallets, as well as several other types. When we look at all of these hammers, they look different because their makers designed them to serve different purposes. A hammer maker precisely designed each hammer to have a certain weight, length, and shape to function for a specific purpose. In a similar way, God designed everything about us so that we could glorify him. God could have designed us like machines or like fictional aliens we see on television, but he did not. God specifically designed each of us spiritually and physically so we could display his qualities and glorify him. God created us through the very first man and woman, and designed us like them.

God's Creation of the First Man

After God created the earth and made it livable, he made the very first man. This is the man from whom we all descend. God created the man by forming a physical body using the elements of the earth. The Scriptures refer to these elements collectively as the "dust," but they are simply the elements which he had made within the earth. After God made the man's body, he caused it to become alive or to become a living soul by breathing into him the breath of life. Genesis 2:7 says, "Then the Lord God formed the man of dust from the ground and breathed into his nostrils the breath of life, and man became a living creature." God's breathing into the man the breath of life is synonymous with God's giving him a spirit. God did not breathe into the man like we do with a balloon. Rather, when God breathed into the man, he gave him a spirit that caused him to become alive. Adam was alive because God made his body from the earth and placed his spirit within it.

God Named the First Man *Adam*

After God made the first man, he named him Adam. God could have named him Richard or Michael, but he named him Adam for a very specific reason. The name Adam is directly related to the general term "man." The first occurrence of the word "man" in the Scriptures is in Genesis 1:26. It says, "Then God said, 'Let us make man in our image.'" The English word "man" in this verse is based on the Hebrew word *a-dam*. When the writer of Genesis 1:26 wrote *a-dam*, he did not include the definite article *ha*, which we translate "the." He wrote "man" without the article because God had only made one man, and this man was alone on the earth. We could accurately translate Genesis 1:26 as, "Let us make a man in our image."

However, God intended to create a woman. So when the writer of Genesis began writing about God's impending creation of a woman he began using the phrase "the man." The phrase "the man" was based on the Hebrew phrase *ha a-dam* with the definite article. God did this to distinguish the first man from the first woman.

As time continued, the first man and the first woman would produce offspring. This again changed how God referred to "the man." God would no longer refer to the first man as "the man" because there would eventually be more men. As such, the writer of Genesis began using the word "man" again, which was *a-dam*, without the definite article. He did this because God had named the first man Adam. *A-dam* was now the proper name Adam and was the first man's proper name. Once Adam began to reproduce with the first woman, God intended all people on the earth to have names. This includes us and is the reason we each have a name. Our names distinguish us from one another.

God's Creation of the First Woman

After God created Adam, he also made a woman. A woman is similar to the man except she has different characteristics than he does so she can complement him. When God made the woman, he did not make her in the same way that he had made the man. Instead, God took part of the man's body, namely a rib, and used it to form her body. This may seem strange to us because God could have made her from the elements of the ground as he did with Adam, but he did not. God specifically made the first woman from Adam's rib because he naturally designed her to be united to him as a partner who complements him. 1 Corinthians 11:8-9 says, "For man was not made from woman, but woman from man. Neither was man created for woman, but woman for man."

We see this concept in everyday life. A person may construct a building out of a certain type of brick. He may then construct another building next to it out of the same brick so that it complements the first building. In a similar way, God made the first man, Adam, from the elements of the ground. He then made the first woman from him so that she complements him. After God formed the woman's body, he also breathed into her the breath of life and gave her a spirit. The Scriptures do not state this explicitly, but we can appropriately infer it.

The First Woman Was Named *Eve*

When God made the woman, he gave her the name Eve. The name Eve is a variation of Hebrew word *hawah* which means "to be" or "to exist." God gave her this name because she would become the mother of all of us who would eventually exist. Genesis 3:20 says, "The man called his wife's name Eve, because she was the mother of all the living." We see that God gave her the proper name Eve in 1 Timothy 2:13-14 which says, "For it was Adam who was first created, and then Eve. And it was not Adam who was deceived, but the woman." This verse mentions the woman along with her proper name.

We Came from Adam and Eve

We all came from Adam and Eve. If we trace our ancestry back, we will eventually end at Adam and Eve as our first parents. We, of course, did not know them, but we still descend from them. We descend from them because when God created Adam and Eve, he had given them the ability to reproduce with each other. In the course of time, Adam and Eve began producing offspring. Each time they did, Adam's reproductive cell united with Eve's reproductive cell. We call the moment when this happened the "moment of conception."

When Adam and Eve produced their first offspring, two things happened. First, God created a new body of a person within Eve's body. The body had roughly half of Adam's physical characteristics and half of Eve's physical characteristics. The person's new body would have had some of the same physical features as Adam and Eve such as facial features, hair color, and skin tone. Second, God also created a new spirit and placed it within the newly created body within Eve's womb. The new spirit within the new body caused Adam and Eve's first offspring to become a living soul. The words "being" or "soul" have the same meaning of "something that is alive or exists." Hosea shows that Adam and Eve's first offspring became a living soul at the moment of conception when it links the three events of birth, pregnancy, and conception. Hosea 9:11 says, "No birth, no pregnancy, no conception!"

We Came from God

Each time Adam and Eve produced offspring, each new person had a body and a spirit. Furthermore, each new person normally had the ability to reproduce in the same way. This cycle of reproduction continued so that every person conceived and born normally had the ability to conceive and bear a new person. This is how we eventually came into being. Because all of us descended from Adam and Eve in this manner, it means God made each of us. When people ask us how we know God made us, we explain that we are offspring of Adam and Eve. Because God made Adam and Eve, he also made us. Hypothetically, if we did not descend from Adam and Eve for whatever reason, God did not make us. There is no existential connection between God and us, and we cannot glorify him. As such, God had to have made us through Adam and Eve.

Our coming from Adam and Eve means we came from God. This may not be anything new to us, but it may be to non-Christians, and it may be problematic for them. Non-Christians do not believe in the true God so they may not believe we came from Adam and Eve. In many cases, they do not even believe Adam and Eve were real people and actually existed. However, non-Christians know we must have come from somewhere. We did not just appear. There must be some explanation regarding where we came from. A prominent explanation which they hold to is called the "theory of evolution." The theory of evolution contrasts the truth regarding how we came into being, but it is not simply an alternative view. It is a common view that directly opposes the truth about how God actually created us.

The Theory of Evolution

According to the theory of evolution, a cosmic event occurred millions of years ago in which all matter in the universe came into being. No one knows, however, the cause of this cosmic event. Proponents of this theory, however, claim it was not God because he does not exist. When this cosmic event produced all the matter in the universe, among this matter were single cell organisms. These single cell organisms contained an inherent natural ability to evolve and self-develop physical and mental traits. As these cells came into a situation or an environment in which they may be destroyed or simply die, they self-developed a trait that caused them to survive. When these single cells reproduced, they passed on to the next generation of cells the trait they had developed.

Over millions of years, these cells evolved in this way to form all living organisms in the universe, including us. At first glance, science seems to support the validity of the theory of evolution. If we look more closely, however, we see that it actually does the opposite.

There are two reasons science does not support the theory of evolution. First, the theory assumes that living beings contain an inherent natural ability to evolve and become more advanced as a means to survive. This, however, is not the case. No one has ever conducted an experiment to prove this basic tenet of the theory of evolution. There are indeed physical changes that occur in us as well as animals, but these are part of our inherent ability to adapt to certain environments such as the skin's ability to tan and the blood's ability to thin. Our ability to adapt, however, is not an inherent natural ability to evolve. Second, the theory of evolution could not have actually happened because it requires such a long amount of time; i.e. billions and billions of years. In order for us as people to actually have come into being based on the evolution of single cell organisms, those cells must have gone through a series of steps. Each of these steps are so random that by the time we would have finally come into being by chance, the sun in the earth's solar system would have burned out.

So, science itself does not support the theory of evolution. The truth is that God created Adam and Eve as the first two people. God then created us from them, and he is no less our creator as he was Adam and Eve's. As such, God gave us the purpose of displaying his qualities of life, knowledge, power, and righteousness so he is glorified.

Our Constitution

We each have a body with a spirit, which forms our souls or lives. This is our constitution. It is inevitable, however, that a book on theology such as this one will mention some rarely used and slightly esoteric words. However, when we discuss our constitution as human beings, i.e. our bodies and spirits, two terms usually emerge; the dichotomous and trichotomous views. We as Christians and even non-Christians discuss our human constitutions using these two words.

The Dichotomous and Trichotomous Views

The dichotomous[5] view teaches that our spirit and our soul are the same thing. Each time the Scriptures use either the word soul or spirit, it is also referring to the other. According to this view, we are composed of a spirit or soul within a body. Adversely, the trichotomous view teaches that our spirit and our soul are distinct. Each time the Scriptures use the word soul, they are speaking of one entity. Each time they use the word spirit, they are speaking of an entirely different entity. According to this view, we are composed of a spirit, a soul, and a body. Because the apparent juxtaposition of these two views, we may think one of them is correct and the other is false. We may then choose to hold to the one we think is right. Before we do this, however, we need to realize that neither of these views are completely correct, but both have aspects that are correct.

There does exist a spirit, a soul, and a body as three separate entities. 1 Thessalonians 5:23 says, "May your whole spirit and soul and body be kept blameless at the coming of our Lord Jesus Christ." When this passage mentions these three entities, it is correct because they all actually exist. However, we are not composed of a spirit, soul, and body. They exist, but we are not composed of them. We are composed of a body and a spirit. James 2:26 says, "For as the body apart from the spirit is dead." The third entity, the soul, is an actual entity, but it is not an entity we are composed of. The soul is synonymous with life or being. We are composed of a spirit and body, which together forms our souls or lives.

We can look at this in a different way. When God made our spirits, our souls were originally with them. When God placed our spirits into our bodies at the moment of conception, our spirits as well as our bodies became a soul. This is why we sometimes call other people "souls." The spirit and the body together form a soul. However, we can also look at this in reverse. When we die, our spirits separate from our bodies, but our souls remain with our spirits. Our spirits are alive just as they were when God made them prior to our conceptions. However, if our spirits also die, our souls will then separate from them as well. This is why Hebrew 4:12 says in reference to the gospel, "Piercing to the division of soul and of spirit." A non-Christian's rejection of the gospel will cause his spirit to die and his soul to separate from it.

---

[5] The word dichotomy comes from the Greek word *dichotomia*, which means "to divide a whole into two parts." The word dichotomy, however, is not accurate as it pertains to a person's constitution. Bipartite would be more accurate because it means "composed of two parts."

The Nature of Our Spirits

Our spirits are a unique entity within each of us. There are many different kinds of spirits. God is one kind of spirit. Satan is another kind of spirit. An angel is a third kind of spirit. Even in the animal world, each animal has a different kind of spirit. A horse has one kind, and a lobster has another kind. We as people have spirits that are different than any other type of spirit. However, all spirits including ours function in similar ways.

Each spirit has an intellect that can think. What we are thinking right now, our spirits our thinking because our spirits contain our intellect.[6] 1 Corinthians 2:11 says, "For who knows a person's thoughts except the spirit of that person, which is in him?" Every thought we have, whether good or bad, our spirits think. Each of our spirits also has a will that makes choices for us. Every decision and choice we have ever made, our spirits made them because our spirits also contain our will. Matthew 26:41 says, "The spirit is indeed willing, but the flesh is weak." As our spirits receive knowledge through our senses, they think about this knowledge and make choices about things pertaining to our well-being.

The Emotional Condition of Our Spirits

In addition to reasoning and making choices, our spirits can also be in various states or conditions. Each of us has been happy, scared, sad, and angry. When we were, it was our spirits[7] that were experiencing these states or conditions. However, our spirits did not motivate themselves to be in a certain condition. Influences outside of us brought about the condition of our spirits. In other words, outside influences moved our spirits to be in the condition they were in. For this reason, we refer to the conditions of our spirits as emotions.

The word emotion comes from the Latin words *ek* and *movere* meaning "moved from outside." We cannot motivate our own spirits to be in the condition they are in. Something outside of ourselves must move them. It could be a person which makes us sad such as when we lose a loved-one. It could also be an event which makes us happy such as our wedding day. Something outside of ourselves must cause our spirits to be in

---

[6] The discipline of psychology is in the Scriptures and pertinent to theology because it deals with the mind or intellect.

[7] For this reason any object that has a spirit can experience emotions. Spiritual beings, people, and even animals can all experience emotions. Plants, rocks, and water cannot experience emotions because they do not have spirits.

a certain condition. We see this in the Scriptures, specifically, Jonah 4:6 and 9. In this passage, God caused a plant to grow up and provide shade for Jonah. As a result, Jonah's spirit was happy about this. However, God caused a worm to destroy the plant so that Jonah did not have any shade. This caused Jonah's spirit to be unhappy so that he asked to die. The things God did with the plant affected the condition of Jonah's spirit.

When outside influences affect the condition of our spirits, these same conditions can in turn affect our bodies. When we hear bad news, our spirits become saddened. Our bodies naturally respond by sighing or make a physical gesture of disappointment. If the news is bad enough, we may need to sit or lie down. Adversely, when we hear good news, our spirits are cheered. Our bodies respond by smiling or our eyes brighten. If the news is good enough, we may jump or dance. This is the reason a coach will give a pep talk to his team before a game. He knows that encouraging his players' spirits will have a direct effect on their physical performance.

God made all of us a little differently, but our differences should not cause us to think that we are more or less inclined to glorify God. We each can glorify God just as much as anyone else. God made us with spirits that think and will. He placed them within our bodies that can speak and act. God made us exactly this way so we would have the capacity to receive from him the qualities of life, knowledge, power, and righteousness. God's giving us this capacity is what it means for God to have made us in his image. Genesis 1:27 says, "So God created man in his own image."

God Created Us in His Image

God's creating us in his image means he created us with the *capacity* to display his glory. God made us with this capacity by giving[8] us a spirit that can live, know, be empowered, and have the qualities of righteousness. Unlike animals whose spirits cannot do this, we as people have spirits with this capacity. God placed each of our spirits within our bodies on the earth so we can have these qualities and glorify him. This view is called the Substantive View because God gives us his four broad qualities, and they are an essential part of who we are.

We can look at the concept of God's creating us in his image in a slightly different way. God made us to be analogical copies of him in earthly form. When someone makes

---

[8] Because God gives us these qualities, we sometimes refer to them as transferrable or communicable qualities.

one object in the image of another object, the two are called analogues. One analog is the genuine original, and the other one is the copy. Someone makes an analogical copy of a genuine object so it has similar qualities as the genuine object and can function in a similar way. A common example of this is synthetic motor oil. We make synthetic motor oil to be analogical copy of genuine motor oil so it has similar qualities and can function in a similar way. In our case, God made us as analogical copies of himself, and we bear his image. We have the capacity to receive his qualities and display his glory.

Some Christians have developed various alternate views of what the image of God means. These views do not necessarily contain false statements, but they do not specifically describe what it means for us to have been made in the image of God. One view is the relational view. According to this view, the image of God is our ability to relate to God. We, unlike anything else in the creation, can talk to God, think about God, and respond to God. According to this view, we have this ability because we have the image of God within us. Another view is the functional view. According to this view, the image of God is our ability to rule over the creation. According to this view, we as people have the exclusive right to rule over the animals, plants, and even ourselves. Genesis 1:26 says, "Let us make man in our image, after our likeness. And let them have dominion over the fish of the sea and over the birds of the heavens." These views, though they contain accurate information about us, do not accurately describe what it means for us to have the image of God. We do indeed have the ability to relate to God, and we also have dominion over the creation. However, our having these two abilities is not tantamount to our being made in the image of God. Our being made in the image of God means God designed us at the substantive level to have a spirit and body with the capacity to display the qualities of life, knowledge, power, and righteousness so we can reflect God's glory.

For years astronauts traveled into space on the Space Shuttle. In order for the Space Shuttle to do this, scientists had to design everything about it very precisely. They had to design the vessel itself to be a certain size, weight, shape, and substance. They could not simply choose it to be a certain shape or choose to make it out of just any kind of metal. They also had to design it to carry a certain number of astronauts. These astronauts could not just take any bag with them like we may do on airplanes. Scientists specifically and carefully designed the Space Shuttle so it would perform its intended purpose. In a similar way, God gave to each of us the grand purpose of glorifying him. For us to do this, he specifically designed and engineered each of us to have a certain kind of spirit and a certain kind of body. With these two entities, God gave us life, knowledge, power, and righteousness on this earth. God's designing us this way enables us to display his glory as the one, true, and magnificent God.

Chapter 3

What Sin Is and How It Affects Us

As Christians, God made each of us with the inherent purpose of glorifying him. We cannot unhinge ourselves from this purpose because God made it part of who we are. We know without a doubt that this is why God made us. As we drive down a country road with no one else around, we know God made us to glorify him. However, we are also very aware that we are sinful. We know we are sinful because the Scriptures tell us we are, but they do not need to. We know we are sinful because we feel sin within us. We feel in our bodies the desire to disobey God and seek our own glory instead of his. The sin within us prevents us from glorifying God, and causes us to fall short. Because sin affects us, we know quite a lot about it. We know when we sin in a thought we think, in a word we speak, or in something we have done. We can articulate to our own shame and disgust that what we just did was sinful and why it was. We also know that we should avoid sin. There is no lack of preachers or even Christians that will tell us when, where, and how to avoid sin. They will also tell us what will happen if we do not avoid it. We know quite a bit about sin. What we may not know, however, is what sin is and how we became sinful.

What Sin Is

Many of us have heard of sin predominantly in the verb form. I.e. sin is something we do that God does not want us to do. Sin, however, is much more than this. Sin is the power within each of us that causes us to disobey God when he teaches us how to glorify him. God's instructions are clear because he makes them clear. No one can ever claim that he did not know how to live or was confused about God's instructions. Sin is not our having a lack of knowledge about what God teaches us. Rather, sin is the power within us that causes us to flagrantly disobey God's clear instructions. Romans 7:20 says, "Now, if I do what I do not want, it is no longer I who do it, but sin that dwells within me." Because of our sin, we think, speak, and act in sinful ways so we glorify ourselves instead of God. God calls all of these thoughts, words, and actions sin because they are the direct effects of sin within us. In other words, the sin within us causes certain effects in our lives and we have named these effects after the cause. We sin because we have sin.

Sin is a real power that God has caused to dwell within us. There is nothing we can do to get sin out of us. There is nothing we can do to keep from being sinful in how we live. We may think we can simply exert will power or modify our behavior to keep from sinning, but we cannot. Any sin that we struggle with, God caused us to struggle with it. There is nothing we can do about it. God made us sinful because we are related to the very first people whom he created, Adam and Eve.

Adam and Eve's Original Sinful Disposition

God created Adam to have sin within him. This may not be a common view among some of us, but it is in fact the case. When God created Adam, he "depraved" him. The concept of "deprave" means "to make sinful." God made Adam sinful as well as Eve whom he created directly from Adam. They were both inclined to sin prior to their committing the first sin because God made them to have sin within them and have a sinful nature.

All animals have a nature. Dogs, whales, and mosquitos all have a nature. Their nature determines what they are inclined to do. We can modify the behavior of some animals, but we do not have the power to change the nature of any animal. Each animal will always be inclined to follow its nature regardless of the level of training and taming we impose on it. In the same way, God made Adam and Eve to have sin within them. As such, they had a sinful nature. Even before Adam and Eve sinned for the first time, they were inclined to sin because God made them with a sinful nature. Romans 11:32 says, "For God has consigned all to disobedience." The word "all" is a reference to all people and includes Adam and Eve. God made Adam and Eve sinful so they would be inclined to follow their sinful nature.

Because God made Adam and Eve sinful, he wanted them to know they were sinful. God made them aware that they were sinful by giving them a command. The command is recorded in Genesis 2:16-17, which says, "And the Lord God commanded the man, saying, 'You may surely eat of every tree of the garden, but of the tree of the knowledge of good and evil you shall not eat, for in the day that you eat of it you shall surely die.'" God gave Adam and Eve this command because he knew they were sinful and would break it. When they broke it, they would then begin to know they were sinful. God's purpose for the tree was to give Adam and Eve a knowledge of good and evil so God named it as such.

One thing some of us may have noticed in the Genesis narrative regarding Adam and Eve's sin is that God only gave Adam the first command. Eve was not even alive when God commanded Adam not to eat from the tree. We can appropriately assume, however, that after God created Eve, Adam told her what the command was so they were both aware of the command. Adam and Eve both[9] chose to disobey God's command and eat from the tree because God made them sinful. When they sinned, this is when sin entered the world. Romans 5:12 says, "Therefore, just as sin came into the world through one man."

Adam and Eve Did Not Have Free Will

Some of us may not have realized that God actually made Adam and Eve sinful. We may have thought that God made Adam and Eve righteous. When they chose to commit the first sin,[10] they caused sin to enter within themselves. As a result, they gave themselves a sinful nature. Many of us have heard this doctrine and accepted it. It may seem noble of us to confess on Adam and Eve's behalf that they made themselves sinful, and God had no part. This, however, is neither right nor necessary.

In order for Adam and Eve to have made themselves sinful, they would have needed to have had a free will. If God did not make them sinful, sin must have entered into them in some way. Sin did not cause itself to enter into Adam and Eve as though it was a contagion on a space ship infecting the crew. So, if hypothetically, God did not create Adam and Eve to have sin within them, sin could only have entered them because Adam and Eve had a free will and allowed sin to enter them.

This is the thing with the concept of free will. It is one of those subjects that is hard to prove or disprove. When we see someone make a choice, whether in the Scriptures or in real life, we cannot easily say that their choice was based on free will or it based on their nature. Christians have argued about this issue for centuries, but our assigning an action as the product of either free will or nature is impossible. The only way we can know for sure which one of these is true is to look at the Scriptures. The Scriptures do not state this explicitly, but they do explain the concept of freedom.

---

[9] This makes sense because Adam and Eve both sinned together. If God had not depraved them, it is very possible that one or both of them may not have sinned.
[10] Some people call the first sin the "original sin." The Scriptures, however, never use this term.

When the Scriptures speak of the concept of freedom, they never speak of it as it pertains to Adam and Eve's wills. They do not even speak of it as it pertains to our wills.[11] The Scriptures speak of freedom as it pertains to numerous things. They speak about a person's freedom from slavery. Exodus 21:5 says, "I will not go out free." They also speak of freedom as it pertains to our freedom from sin. Romans 6:18 says, "Having been set free from sin." The Scriptures speak of freedom in other ways, but they never speak of it as it pertains to anyone's will,[12] including and especially Adam and Eve's. The truth is that Adam and Eve did not have free wills, and they did not make themselves sinful. Rather, God made Adam and Eve sinful when he initially created them. The fact that God created Adam and Eve sinful may cause chagrin with some of us. Even after an unsuccessful search in the Scriptures to find that Adam and Eve made themselves sinful, some of us still have some questions that lurk and fester within us.

Two Questions Regarding Adam and Eve's Sinfulness

One of the first questions, pertains to the word "good." The Scriptures teach us that God made Adam and Eve good. Genesis 1:31 says, "And God saw everything that he had made, and behold, it was very good." If God created Adam and Eve good, how could he have made them sinful? In the Genesis 1:31 passage, the English word "good" is a translation of the Hebrew word *tube*. *Tube* means pleasing or acceptable. God made the systems of the world such as the sun and clouds, the various animals, and us to be pleasing and acceptable to him. We see this even in the New Testament. 1 Timothy 4:4 says, "Everything created by God is good." The word "everything" in this verse is a reference to things in the world at the time when 1 Timothy was written. In this world, like in the world of Genesis, God created everything to be pleasing and acceptable to him for the purpose of glorifying him.

Furthermore, when the Scripture writers explain that God made everything good, they do not mean to say that these things are sinless. God did not create the light and the water as recorded in Genesis as well as the food mentioned in 1 Timothy to be sinless. These things are not moral agents and are not capable of having sin or committing sin. God made Adam and Eve sinful, but they were still good. God made us sinful, but we are still good. 1 Timothy 4:4 is correct when it says everything created by God is good.

---

[11] God is the only being that has a free will.
[12] The concept of free will is like the Bigfoot of the Scriptures. People claim it exists, but they have never seen it and cannot prove it exists.

Everything is indeed good because God made everything pleasing and acceptable to him as he uses it to glorify him.

A second question pertains to God's nature. If God created Adam and Eve to be sinful, does it not imply that God himself is sinful? It does not, and it should not. God's making Adam and Eve sinful and causing them to sin does not make God himself sinful or evil. The cause of an effect does not necessarily share the same qualities as the effect. If a pie-maker makes a pie, but he purposely leaves out an ingredient, the quality of the pie is bad. However, this does not mean the pie-maker is a bad pie-maker. Likewise, when God created Adam and Eve sinful, it does not mean he himself is sinful.

None of us should have qualms about God creating Adam and Eve sinful because even today God makes all of us sinful from birth. He also holds us over into disobedience until he gives us faith. God, however, is not sinful because he does this to us. He is certainly not sinful because he did the same with Adam and Eve. God's depraving Adam and Eve and making them sinful should not cause us to be uncomfortable. This idea may not have been an idea we grew up hearing or an idea we have heard before, but it is soundly Scriptural. God did indeed make Adam and Eve sinful, but he did so for a very important purpose. God made them sinful…so we would be sinful. We are directly related to Adam and Eve. Adam and Eve lived many centuries before us, but we still have a direct relationship to them as it pertains to sin.

We Are Sinful Like Adam and Eve

As a result of God making Adam and Eve sinful, he would also make sinful any offspring who descended from them. He would make them sinful so they would be made in the "likeness" of Adam and Eve. Romans 5:19 says, "For as by [because of] the one man's disobedience the many were made sinners." At the moment when each of us is conceived, God would make our bodies to contain sin and place a sinful spirit within each of them. God would do this for every person ever conceived on the earth. This is why David, who was 34 generations from Adam and Eve, said in Psalm 51:5, "Behold, I was brought forth in [with] iniquity, and in [with] sin did my mother conceive me." God makes all of us sinful in the likeness of Adam and Eve. This view is called the Likeness or Representative view.

There are several false views that stand in stark contrast to the Likeness view. The difference between the Likeness view and these false views is in *how* God makes us sinful. We know that Adam had sin within him and was sinful. We also know that we have sin within us and are sinful. Romans 5:19 connects Adam's sin to our sin when it says, "by [because of] the one man's [Adam's] disobedience the many [all of us] were made sinners." The Likeness view explains this connection by asserting that God made us sinful so we would be like sinful Adam. There are, however, three false views that connect our sin to Adam's sin a little differently.

False View #1: Bad Example View

The first view is called the Bad Example view. According to this view, Adam's sin has absolutely no effect on us. We were righteous when we were born because God made each of us to have a righteous spirit within a righteous body. In other words, every person was perfect when they were born, including us. Our spirits had a free will, and we could either choose to sin or not choose to sin. We were not pressured or influenced either way. However, when someone ultimately[13] influenced or pressured us to sin, we sinned and allowed sin to enter us. We supernaturally made our righteous bodies and spirits sinful by allowing sin to enter us. God then ascribed or imputed[14] to us the status of being sinful and guilty[15] because we actually became sinful. This leads to the second view.

False View #2: Natural Headship View

The second view is called the Natural Headship view. According to this view, we were sinful when we were born because our spirits and bodies were inside Adam. When Adam sinned, we sinned along with him though not willfully. When we were all eventually born at some point, we had sinful spirits and sinful bodies. God ascribed or imputed to us the status of being sinful and guilty because we were actually sinful. This leads to a third view.

False View #3: Inheritance View

The third view is called the Inheritance view. According to this view, we were sinful when we were born because Adam transferred his sin to us through inheritance. Adam was sinful, and the seed in his body contained sin within it. Likewise, Eve was sinful, and the eggs in her body contained sin within them. When Adam and Eve produced offspring, they transferred sin to them, similar to how they transferred their genes. Each

---

[13] According to this view, there are actually perfect people on the earth. Some have been born, but have not yet sinned.
[14] "To impute" means "to ascribe" or "to attribute." We can see this in classic American literature.
[15] Guilty means "worthy of being punished."

of their offspring then had a sinful spirit and sinful body. When their offspring produced offspring, they also transferred their sin to them. When we were all eventually born at some point, we had sinful bodies and sinful spirits. God ascribed or imputed to us the status of being sinful and guilty because we were actually sinful.

The fact that these three views are false should not cause us too much consternation because the Scriptures do not support them. Though we may have entertained them, and even casually claimed we held to them, we could never state convincingly that the Scriptures teach them. The Scriptures do teach that people are sinful because God made them in the likeness of sinful Adam who represented them. Hosea 6:7 says, "But like Adam they transgressed the covenant." Even in spite of this, the fact that God purposely made us sinful in Adam's likeness is hard to accept. It may be easier to accept the fact that we freely sinned and we are to blame for our sin. As such, there is still one last exercise we can do to see that the Likeness view is correct. We can analyze it in reverse. In other words, we can understand how we became sinful by analyzing how we became righteous.

We Can Understand Adam by Understanding Christ

When we who were naturally sinful received faith in Christ, we followed Christ in the likeness of his death. Romans 6:5 says, "For if we have been united with him in a death like his." When we followed Christ, our naturally sinful spirits died. This is what it means for us to be crucified with Christ. We were not crucified physically, but we were spiritually because our spirits died. God then remade our spirits in the likeness of Christ's spirit. Through the work of Christ, God regenerated our naturally sinful spirits so they actually became righteous spirits. God made our spirits righteous because he caused us to be remade *in the likeness* of Christ. God did not make us righteous because we followed Christ's good example. God also did not make us righteous because our spirits we were inside Christ, and he gave us righteous spirits when he remade them. Lastly, God did not make us righteous because we inherited righteousness from Christ who was our physical relative. Rather, God made us righteous because he made us in the likeness of Christ and gave us righteous spirits. To reverse this and apply it to our sinfulness, God made us sinful because he made us in the likeness of sinful Adam.

God Made Us Natural Born Sinners

If a person has an old antique coin and wants to find out what kinds of metal it is composed of, he can use an alloy tester to find out. He can simply place the end of the tester on the coin and push the button. The alloy tester will tell him the kinds of metal his coin is made of and the various percentages of each metal. In a similar, but hypothetical way, when we were born, if we each had a sin tester and placed it on our chests, it would indicate that both our spirits and bodies were sinful. They were sinful because God made us in the likeness of Adam. We were natural born sinners.

This may sound harsh, but it is reality. There is nothing we can do to change how we were born. We cannot go back and make ourselves be born without sin. We cannot change our natural make-up. Our parents conceived each of us with sin inside us that affects both our spirits and bodies. We grow up engaging in various types of sins. We think about sinning, we say sinful words, and commit sinful acts. It does not matter where we are and who we are with, we sin because we have sin inside of us. Ephesians 4:17-19 says, "You must no longer walk as the Gentiles do, in the futility of their minds. They are darkened in their understanding...They have become callous and have given themselves up to sensuality, greedy to practice every kind of impurity."

The Effects of Sin in Us

Because we are natural born sinners, sin affects in different ways. It is similar to a virus within a computer. The virus affects the computer in different ways. It affects how the software runs. It affects what we can do with the hardware. It affects what we can use the computer for in our lives. The one virus can have many different effects. Because we are natural born sinners, our sin affected us in three different ways.

We Were in Bondage to Sin

The sin within us affected us so that we were in bondage to it. We were each born with a spirit and a body. Our spirits thought about and made choices, and our bodies carried it out. This is how God made us to function regardless of whether we were righteous or sinful. Because our spirits and bodies were sinful, we were bound to think about, choose, and carry out sin. We were in bondage to sin, and it controlled us. Romans 7:14 says, "I am of the flesh, sold under sin." From birth, sin controlled us so we engaged in all the various kinds of sin. Galatians 5:19-21 says, "Now the works of the flesh are evident: sexual immorality, impurity, sensuality, idolatry, sorcery, enmity, strife, jealously, fits of anger, rivalries, dissensions, divisions, envy, drunkenness, orgies, and things like these." Sin controlled us so that we were forced to acquire something for ourselves that brought glory to us instead of to God. The thing we sought to acquire may have been tangible such as a material possession, or it may have been intangible such as a position of power. There was nothing we could have done to overcome the power of the natural sin within us.[16] It was our nature to sin. The only way for us to have become freed from our sinful nature and its power over us was for God to have redeemed us.

We Were Vitiated by Sin

The sin within us also affected us so that we were vitiated by it. Our being vitiated by sin meant we were impaired so that we could not glorify God in how we lived. Sin impaired our spirits so that we did not and could not think about how to glorify God. Instead, we reasoned through a particular sin and thought about how to maximize our own glory and pleasure. Romans 7:8 and 11 says, "But sin…produced in me all kinds of covetousness." Sin also impaired our bodies so they passionately desired to sin. Our bodies craved to sin like they craved water on a hot day. In several examples, our sinful bodies want more food than we need, they want to say words that kill, they want to think about women other than our wives. Romans 7:23, "I see in my members another law waging war against the law of my mind and making me captive to the law of sin that dwells in my members." Our bodies are vitiated by sin, and we could not overcome our vitiated sinful state on our own. In the same way that a deaf or blind person cannot heal themselves on their own and remove the impairment, we could not overcome our vitiated state on our own. The only way for us to have overcome sin was for God to have cleansed us.

We Are in Debt to God

Lastly, the sin within us affected us so that we were in debt to God. Each time we sinned, God recorded it as a debt in our spiritual account, which he maintained in Heaven. God also assigned each of our sins a degree of seriousness. Some sins were less serious, while others were more serious. We see this when Jesus compared Pilate to Judas in John 19:11 which says, "He who delivered me over to you has the greater sin." When God recorded our sin in each of our spiritual accounts, he recorded them with a degree of seriousness. Each sin we committed, regardless of severity, caused us to have guilt or be guilty.[17] Our being guilty meant we were under God's condemnation for

---

[16] A person sins because he is bound to, not because he freely chooses to. A person cannot be both bound to sin and freely choose to do it.

[17] Guilt and shame are not the same things. When we are guilty, we are in a state where we are worthy to be punished. When we have shame or are ashamed, we feel or sense the guilt. For this reason, people may be guilty, but they do not feel ashamed.

our sin, and we were worthy to be punished. When we eventually die and arrive at God's throne on the Day of Judgment, God will review the sins in each of our spiritual accounts. He would have then judged us as guilty of those sins, and we would have had to pay God the total accrued debt for every sin we had ever committed. Romans 4:7 says, "Blessed are those whose lawless deeds are forgiven, and whose sins are covered; blessed is the man against whom the Lord will not count his sin." The only way we could have exempted ourselves from God's requirement to pay our debt of sin was if God forgave us and cancelled our debt.

Our being natural born sinners was a dismal situation for us to be in. Our being in bondage to sin that prevents us from living the way we were made to, only to know that we will be punished for every single sin we ever commit was the most dismal situation we could imagine. However, it would have been even more dismal if we did not know we were in it. We would have been no different than the frog in a pot of water that was getting hotter. If we did not know we were sinful, we would never have taken any steps to deal with our sin. The thing is, we did know we were sinful because God showed us that we were.

How We Knew We Were Sinful

As natural born sinners, everything about our lives was to please and glorify ourselves. Each day when we awoke and went about our business, we constantly sinned. We spoke to others sinfully. We ate sinfully. We spent our money sinfully. We did many things in the course of our day that were sinful. We were always looking for ways to obtain glory and pleasure for ourselves. We did these things because God allowed Satan to tempt us. Satan tempted us by using our sinful passions or appetites to entice us to receive a benefit or pleasure that God had not entitled us to receive. James 1:14 says, "But each person is tempted when he is lured and enticed by his own desire." Satan made us perceive that we needed to have these passions or appetites satisfied. As Satan tempted us, God imposed various commands on us at different times in our lives to reveal we had sin within us. In other words, God used Satan's temptation in conjunction with his commands.

God had begun imposing commands on Adam and Eve and continued with others such as Noah, Abraham, and Jacob to show them they had sin within them. God continued to do this until he gave the Israelites the Law. When God gave the Old Covenant Law, but before he gave the Holy Spirit, the Israelites knew they were sinful through the commands of the law. The commands addressed various issues in their daily lives. Romans 7:7 says, "If it had not been for the law, I would not have known sin." When an Israelite heard a particular command of the law, it revealed to him that he was sinful in some regard. God designed the law, however, to only be applicable until the Holy Spirit came.

After Jesus' death and resurrection, God sent the Holy Spirit who replaced the Law. The Holy Spirit began doing within us one of the things the law had previously done to God's people. The Holy Spirit showed us we sin. Romans 2:14 says, "When Gentiles, who do not have the law, by nature do what the law requires, instinctively the things of the Law, these, not having the Law, are a law to themselves in that they show the work of the Law written in their hearts, their conscience bearing witness." Our conscience is a function within our spirit that makes us aware[18] of our sin. The Holy Spirit worked through our conscience, and convinced us that we had sin within us. Each of us knew what sin was and when we committed it.

The Holy Spirit Shows Us Our Motive and Intent

When a person commits a crime and is caught by the police, he may not admit to the crime. He does not want to admit to anyone that he is a bad person and committed a shameful act. However, the police may try to help him admit to it by showing him his motive and intent. When they do, he realizes who he is and what he did. In a similar way, the Holy Spirit did more than non-audibly tell us that we were sinning. He certainly told us we were sinning, but as he did it, he also informed us of our motive and intent. We knew we were sinners and what we wanted to get by sinning.

Everything we do involves a concept called motive. Our motive in doing any act is was what drove us to do the act. Our desire for nutrition motivated us to eat. Our desire to earn an income motivated us to go to work. Everything we think, say, and do involves a motive. This, however, is only half of the equation. Everything we do also involves a concept called intent. Our intent in doing any act is what we wanted to accomplish. Our goal in showering is to clean our bodies. Our goal in sending a birthday card to a family member is to show our devotion. Everything we think, say, and do also involves intent.

Because we were natural born sinners, we had a motive and intent to do every sin. Sin motivated us to think specific thoughts, say specific words, and do specific actions with the specific intent of obtaining a certain type of pleasure and glory for ourselves.

---

[18] The word conscience is a cognate of the word conscious which means aware.

Whenever we sinned, the Holy Spirit informed us of our sin, along with our motive and intent, in order that we would be fully aware that we were sinning, the reason we were sinning, and what we wanted to get by sinning.

God Punishes Those Who Remain Natural Born Sinners

The Holy Spirit goes to this length to inform us of our sin so we are fully aware that we should not do it. Some of us Christians may think at times that we have a right to sin. We do not. We do not have a right to say whatever we want to others, even if they say whatever they want to us. We do not have a right to take something that we are not entitled to have, even if others are taking it. We do not have a right to sin in any way. Adversely, we have an obligation to do what is right. In all circumstances, at all times, in all places, and with all people, God requires and expects that we do the right thing. If we do not, God will punish us when we die.

If we had remained natural born sinners, we would have faced punishment as our dim future. It would have involved the death of our bodies and eventually our spirits. God would have caused our spirits to die as punishment for our sin because they never fulfilled the purpose for which God made them. Our deaths would then serve to vindicate God and show that he deserved to be glorified. Deuteronomy 32:41 says, "I will take vengeance on my adversaries and will repay those who hate me." The phrase "take vengeance" or "get revenge" means "to impose punishment on someone for purposes of vindication." At the Judgment, God would have taken vengeance on us because of our sin and imposed a penalty of death. We would have had to pay this penalty for eternity because as natural born sinners we would have never glorified God.

There Is Only One Way to Overcome Sin

One thing we may have never realized about the universe is that everything in it is broken. We may think otherwise until we realize that nothing in the universe will last forever. Logic teaches us that if God made something to exist it should never cease to exist. If it ceases to exist, then it is broken. This is the case with everything God made, including us. God made us, but he made us naturally sinful, and we are broken. We cannot display God's qualities of life, knowledge, power, and righteousness in a full amount. As such, we cannot glorify him, and he will cause us to die. This cannot be all there is to God's work in making us. Certainly, God did not just give us limited lives, knowledge, power, and righteousness only to take them and cause us to come to nothing. He did not. There is more to God's work than this, much more.

Chapter 4

Why God Limits Our Lives and We Die

A master chess player is very different than a novice chess player. Both types of players move the pieces around the board, and both have the same goal. A master chess player, however, engages in certain practices that the novice does not. He moves his pieces, gives them up, and uses them to coordinate attacks all in total unison with each other. Because of the master chess player's experience, he is not usually caught off guard by his opponent's next move. God is similar, but more so, and perfectly so. God made us to glorify him, but he also made us to be naturally sinful. We cannot glorify God in our current sinful state. God, however, knows exactly what he is doing. God did not give us life just to punish us with death. He had a very specific purpose in giving us life and in how he brought us to the point where we live today.

God Is Life

The one true God is not simply alive. He is life and is the source of all life. Everything that is alive came from God and received its life from him. We, as people, have life because God gave us life. Every beat of our hearts, every blink of our eyes, and every breath we take occurs because God gave us life. Ecclesiastes 8:15 says, "The days of his life that God has given him under the sun." When the Scriptures speak of our lives, they use the Hebrew words *chay* and *nephesh*, and the Greek words *zoei* and *psuchei*. All four of these words have the basic meaning of *existence* or *life*. None of us would be alive unless God made us to live and gave us life. In accordance with God's plan to give us life, he created the universe and the livable earth within it as a place for us to live. God created them in two stages.

Stage One: From Nothing to a Formless and Empty Earth

The first stage begins with nothing. At one point in the history of the universe, nothing existed besides God himself. This may be kind of hard to understand, but it is true. At one point, everything we see and experience daily did not exist. God, however, began his work. In the first stage, God created the heavens and a formless and empty earth. Genesis 1:1 says, "In the beginning, God created the heavens and the earth." Modern parlance uses the word "universe" to describe the heavens and the earth even though the Scriptures do not. The word universe, however, accurately explains God's creation because the word *uni* comes from the Latin word *unus* meaning "one," and the word *verse* comes from the Latin word *versus*[19] meaning "rotating" or "turning." The universe is composed of numerous cosmological bodies all rotating around other cosmological bodies in a small rotating system. All of these smaller rotating systems are part of larger rotating systems,[20] and they all are in sync with each other.

God created the universe by commanding it to come into existence from within himself without using any preexisting matter. Though the Genesis account does not say the universe came into being by God's commanding it, Psalm 33:6 says, "By the word of the Lord the heavens were made, and by the breath of his mouth all their host."

The above description is not the common view. It may sound a little like it, but it is not exactly what many of us have learned. The common view many of us have learned is called *ex nihilo*. Ex nihilo is a Latin phrase translated "from[21] nothing." According to ex nihilo, God created everything from nothing, not from himself. The ex nihilo view is based on a verse from the Catholic Scriptures, namely, 2 Maccabees 7:28 that says, "I beg you, child, to look at the heavens and the earth and see all that is in them; then you will know that God did not make them out of existing things."

However, the ex nihilo view is not accurate even though it seems so. The view that God made everything from nothing as its source is false. The source of everything that exists is not from nothing. Everything and anything must come from something that already exists. At the initial creation, God was the only entity that existed so everything must have come from him. Even the Protestant Scriptures themselves teach that God is the source of the universe. The Protestant Scriptures say in Hebrews 11:3, "By faith we understand that the universe was created by the word of God, so that what is seen was not made out of things that are visible." The implication is that what is seen did not come from the material already in the universe, but rather from God himself. God created everything from himself, not from nothing because from nothing, nothing comes, but from something, something comes. At the initial creation, God himself was the only entity that existed, and everything came from him.

---

[19] The word *versus* used in legal or sports settings means *turned against*.
[20] Everything is likely rotating around the one point in the universe where God caused all matter to come into existence.
[21] The word *ex* in Latin pertains to source and should be translated "from."

The Very First Point in Time and Space

At the moment when God called all physical matter into existence from himself, this was the very first point in time and space. There was no other place else besides this place. There was no time before this time. Prior to this time and place, the only entity that existed was God himself. When God called the basic matter that composes all things into existence, everything and anything that is part of the physical universe began.[22] The very molecules that make up the taste buds in our mouths or the dust on the surface of the moon, God created at this time and in this place. When God called all matter into existence, it began to expand and continued to expand for millions of years until God formed one particular arrangement of matter at a particular place in the universe. This arrangement of matter was our earth. Genesis 1:1 says, "In the beginning, God created the heavens and the earth." In the Old Testament, the most prominent word for "earth" is the Hebrew word *erets*. In the New Testament, it is *ge*. Both words mean "lands."

When we hear that God caused all matter to expand for millions of years, including and especially the earth, we may wonder why. God did this because he was forming all the necessary components within the earth for us. God could have caused the earth in its current state to simply come into existence, but he did not. Every material within the entire earth God created over long amounts of time so it could serve us in some way as we lived on it. This accords perfectly with the anthropic principle. The anthropic principle teaches that God created a finely tuned universe and earth so we could exist. Any minute deviation in how God made the universe and the earth would prevent us from existing.

Even though God prepared the earth for us in this manner, it was initially formless and empty. Genesis 1:2 says, "The earth was without form and void." We could not have lived on this formless and empty earth. The earth would have been like a house that simply had the wooden beams constructed on a foundation. When God made us, we would not have survived on it for very long. God, however, was not completed with his work yet. He would still do certain things during a second stage to make the earth livable for us.

---

[22] Some Christians may consider this the Big Bang. However, the official scientific theory called the Big Bang includes many different aspects which may not be compatible with the Scriptures or even reality.

Stage Two: From a Formless and Empty Earth to a Livable Earth

In the second stage, God made the formless and empty earth into a livable earth for us. He did this by commanding the necessary life sustaining systems to come into existence on the earth. This is sometimes called "Fiat Creationism" because the Latin word *fiat* means "command without further effort." God commanded these life sustaining systems to come into existence through a series of creative acts that he carried out over six consecutive twenty-four-hour days.[23] God made the earth livable in six days because the Scriptures use a number to indicate that God established a particular system on a certain day. God also carried out his creative acts in twenty-four-hour days because the Scriptures use the phrase, "there was evening and there was morning" to show that each day was roughly the same amount of time as a modern twenty-four-hour period.

When God made the earth livable, he had us in mind. God systematically made the earth livable in a manner so that we could readily inhabit it. The way God made the earth livable is similar to how we make an aquarium live-able for new fish. We prepare the aquarium with all the necessary items. When we arrive with the fish, we carefully acclimate them to the aquarium. We do this for the benefit of the fish. God did the same when he made the earth livable for us.

God made the earth livable for us by commanding the necessary life sustaining systems to come into existence in the proper order for our benefit. God did not create them arbitrarily. He created them in a specific order, which Genesis 1 gives. It is important to keep in mind that the Genesis 1 account is a non-scientific explanation. Though the Scriptures and specifically Genesis give completely true and accurate information, God did not intend that they address scientific issues. God intended them to give a brief description so we can understand the specific order in which God made the earth livable for us.

Genesis teaches that the formless and empty earth in its primordial state was a rock with soil that contained only water on its surface. On day one, God created non-luminary light[24] which also included heat. The light and heat caused evaporation of the water on the earth. On day two, God created the clouds in the air and bodies of water on the earth which could be sustained by the former system. The existence of clouds,

---

[23] The word "day" in the Old Testament is the word *yoam* which has three prominent meanings. It can mean a period equivalent to a modern twenty-four-hour period, a period equivalent to modern one-year period, or indefinite period. In Genesis 1, it means a period equivalent to a modern twenty-four-hour period.

[24] Non-luminary light is the kind of light that will exist on the new earth.

however, did not indicate the existence of rain because the water on the earth came up from the ground. Genesis 2:5-6 says, "The Lord God had not caused it to rain on the land, and there was no man to work the ground, and a mist was going up from the land and was watering the whole face of the ground." On day three, God created vegetation under the dirt which when grown could be sustained by the light, heat, and water which God had already created.

On day four, God created the sun, moon, and stars to regulate the previously created systems. When God created the sun, the light from the sun replaced God's non-luminary light. On day five, God created some of the animals as part of the ecosystem. God would use these animals to sustain the inhabited earth. On day six, God created other animals as part of the ecosystem, as well as the first man to rule over it. God created all of these life-sustaining systems for us so we could live on the earth and glorify God. God then rested on the seventh day, but not because he needed physical rest.

This view is called "Two Stage Creationism" because God made the earth we live on today in two stages. The two-stage creation view seems to some of us to be in accord with both Scripture and science. In fact, it explains how we and the earth came into being and does not contradict scientific fact or a correct interpretation of Scripture. However, some people do not believe it. For various reasons, they do not accept the basic interpretation of Genesis 1. They do not believe that when God created the heavens and the earth, he did so over a period of millions of years, and then proceeded to make it livable in six consecutive twenty-four-hour days. As a result, they have created alternative views. There are several alternative views, but two of them are popular. One of these two holds that the earth is actually millions of years old. We call this an "old earth view." The other view holds that the earth is actually about six thousand years old, but only appears millions of years old. We call this a "new earth view."

False View: Day Age View

According to the Day Age view, God created the formless and empty earth millions of years ago. This is the earth mentioned in Genesis 1:1. God began making this earth livable in six consecutive days, each of which was millions of years in duration. God completed his work in making it livable about six thousand years ago.

False View: Ideal Time View

According to the Ideal Time view, God created the formless and empty earth about six thousand years ago immediately prior to day one. God then proceeded to make the earth livable in six consecutive twenty-four days. God did both things in such a way that the earth today would have the inherent appearance and substantive composition of having been created millions of years ago even though he created it only six thousand years ago.

These views are false because they do not reflect what happened. God created the earth millions of years ago so it developed with all the necessary elements and properties to sustain life such as minerals, oil, and metals, among many other things. God then used these elements to make the earth livable in six consecutive days so we could live on it and glorify him. This is the earth God made for us, and he made it exactly how he intended it.

The World We Live in

When we speak about living on the earth, we sometimes say that we live in the world. This raises the issue of whether the earth and the world are the same thing. They are not. When the Scriptures speak of God's creation of the world such as in Romans 1:20 which says, "Having been clearly perceived, ever since the creation of the world," they are not speaking of the created earth. The earth we *live on* and the world we *live in* are closely related, but there is a fine distinction. The earth is the physical planet God made for us to live on. It consists of rock, dirt, water, plants, and animals, among other things. The book of Genesis uses the word earth often because it pertains to the creation of the physical planet we live on. The world, on the other hand, is the people on the earth. We who make up the collective society of all people on the earth and how we interact with each other are the world. The Hebrew word for world is *tebel*, meaning "inhabited," and the Greek word is *cosmos*, meaning "order."

The world we live in is characterized by sin because the people of the world are sinful. As such, when the Scriptures speak of the world, they often do so with a sinful or negative nuance. They do not always speak of the world as simply people who interact with each other through customs, cultures, and manners. They speak of the world as people who interact with each other sinfully. For this reason, we often use the phrase, "The way of the world" to describe how the world works. Though God created the world to be characterized by sin, he still provides for all of us the things we need to live. At times throughout history, the world in which we live became more sinful. At other times, the world in which we live became less sinful. However, regardless of how sinful the world became at any given moment, God has always provided for us the things we need to live. We call this *Providence*.

Providence

After God created a livable earth, he did not continue to establish it. After the sixth day of his making the earth livable, God rested and was done. He did, however, continue to work by taking care of the world that lived on the earth. He did this through *providence*. The concept of providence entails God's care and maintenance over us as we live on the earth. Through providence, God as our Father gives to each of us our basic necessities as well as the things that give us a certain quality of life. Acts 14:17 says, "He did good by giving you rains from heaven and fruitful seasons, satisfying your hearts with food and gladness." The focus of God's providence is on his giving us the things we need, not his creating them. We see this in the analogy of a father and his children. When a father provides his children with food, he gives them the right kind of food, the right amount of food, and gives it to them at the right time for their health. The father's provision of food to his children has nothing to do with where or how he obtained the food. In a similar way, God's providence to us pertains to his giving us everything we need to stay alive, but also the things that make us happy and allow us to enjoy the lives he gave us. When God gives us money so we can take a summer vacation, this is just as much a part of God's providence as when he provides us with food on our table. God provides each of us with different things that sustain us and allow us to enjoy our lives. God exercises his providence in several different ways.

One way God provides for us is through giving us knowledge pertaining to what we need from the earth. Every material thing we have comes from the earth. Every house, vehicle, and piece of furniture comes from the earth. God exercises his providence by giving us knowledge about what we need from the earth. We know what foods we need to eat. We know what types of elements we can use for energy. We may read about God's providence in secular magazines, but it is still God's providence. We have knowledge about what we need because God gave it to us in some form in the course of his providing what we need to live and be happy.

Another way God provides for us is through technology. Technology is the science of how we acquire and manage the material goods from the earth. God gives us the knowledge pertaining to all technological advances so we can acquire every material good that he wants us to have. When God gave us the knowledge about gasoline, he also gave us the knowledge about how to get it and refine it so we can use it. When we think about all the research done in universities and businesses, we may not think that God is active in this, but he is. All knowledge we have about technology comes from God. He gives it to us as part of his providence. God provides for us in other ways, but in every way, God sustains us so we can glorify him.

We Will Eventually Die

God's providence to us will end though because we have sin within us. Each day, we experience all the things God gives us, but eventually he will cease giving us these things on this earth because he did not design us to live forever. He made us so that we would have sin within us, fail to glorify him, and die. There may be differing views on this, but God did not originally create Adam and Eve or any of their offspring to live eternally on the current earth. God created us to be inclined to sin, to act on our sinful inclinations, and eventually die. 1 Corinthians 15:22 says, "For as in [with] Adam all die." As a result, beginning with Adam and Eve, God will take each of our lives at a time specific to each of us.

What Happens When We Die

Most of us are aware that we will die. Though there is nothing we can do about it, we may live in such a way as to delay this as much as we can. The fact remains, however, that we will die because we are naturally sinful. Hebrews 9:27 says, "It is appointed for men to die once." Everything and anything that is sinful must die. This is a bedrock principle that permeates all of theology. When we die, God causes our bodies to cease to function. God may cause our bodies to cease functioning in many ways so that there are numerous causes of death, but behind them all is God who causes our bodies to cease functioning. When our bodies cease to function, our spirits separate from them. James 2:26 says, "The body apart from the spirit is dead." Our bodies then begin to decompose and return to the earth. The decomposition process may be speeded up or slowed down due to various factors, but eventually our bodies return to the dust.

God Will End of the Earth

God has caused even this earth to pass away. When God originally created the earth, he did not design it to last forever. He did not design anything in the current sinful age to last forever. He did not create the cosmological bodies to exist forever and continue to expand infinitely. He did not create the sun to burn forever. He did not create the earth to sustain us forever. When we think about this, it makes absolute sense. God placed us on the earth, but we could not live on it indefinitely. We need certain things from the earth to live, but some of these things cannot be replaced. When we use them up, they are gone, and we cannot get them back. Eventually, the earth will not have enough obtainable resources to sustain us. God has also caused even this earth to pass away. God shows this fact in how he created the earth. He created the earth in six days and rested on the seventh. He could have created the earth in six days, and that would have been it. This may have resulted in our having six-day weeks throughout history. However, God created the earth in six days *and* rested on the seventh. This indicated that the current earth would pass away, and there would be a new earth.

God Gives Us New Life through Christ

If our sinful bodies do not last forever, and the earth we live on does not last forever, there must be something beyond this life. Certainly, God did not transfer life to us, only to take it so we become nothing. Though God made our bodies sinful and we will eventually die, he also made our spirits new and righteous because of Jesus Christ. Jesus Christ came into the naturally sinful world to die and rise from the dead to new life. He died and rose for all of us. When we followed him, our sinful spirits that were in our naturally sinful bodies died with him. We surrendered our sinful spirits and gave up our lives. Luke 9:24 says, "For whoever would save his life will lose it, but whoever loses his life for my sake will save it."

Our giving up our sinful lives and dying with Christ was the most life changing experience we would ever have because our spirits would not stay dead. When our naturally sinful spirits died with Christ, God raised them up and made them new and righteous spirits. When God gave us new spirits, he also gave us new lives. We were no longer who we used to be. God made us righteous and part of his righteous kingdom. Being righteous and part of God's kingdom means we will live forever.

Why We Needed to Turn to Christ

When we think about natural disasters, we often think they are bad. People die. People lose property. The government has to provide basic needs. Everyone pays for the damage in some way. If we think about it though, God causes them. Natural disasters do not happen because of earthly anomalies. They ultimately happen because God causes them to for a good reason. God caused the Flood, he caused Israel to be almost totally consumed, and he will cause every tribulation mentioned in Revelation for a good reason. God causes them so he can rebuild. God intended to make us sinful and curse the earth we live on for good reason. He did not make us to live forever, and he did not make the earth to last forever. This may sound like God made a mistake, but he did not. God designed us this way so he could destroy everything that is sinful and begin again. God began again through Jesus Christ. Through Jesus Christ, God made us new and righteous so we can glorify him forever. John 3:16 says, "For God so loved the world, that he gave his only Son, that whoever believes in him should not perish, but have eternal life."

Chapter 5

Why God Limits Our Knowledge of Him

Some of us have worked several jobs over the course of our lives. In some of our jobs, we had a supervisor who we did not know. We knew who he was, but he was out of sight, and not very involved in our lives as his workers. At first this may have seemed nice, but this kind of relationship usually caused problems. If we needed to know what to do or how to do it, we had to figure it out on our own and did not always make the right choices. In other jobs, however, we had a supervisor who we did know. We knew him and how he wanted things done. If an occasion arose in which we needed guidance, we knew we could just ask him, and he would tell us. We were then able to perform our jobs well. In a similar way, God gave us life on this earth so we could glorify him, but we did not know how to do it. We did not know who God was and we certainly did not know how he wanted us to live so we could glorify him. God specifically limited our knowledge of him so he could make himself known to us. When God made himself known to us, he would give us all the knowledge we needed to glorify him.

God Is Knowledge

God can give us all the knowledge we need because he is knowledge and has a complete understanding of all things. This includes teaching us about who he is and how we can live for his glory. Job 37:16 says, "Do you know the balancings of the clouds, the wondrous works of him who is perfect in knowledge?" The Hebrew words for knowledge are *daath* and *yada,* and the Greek word is *gnosis*. All three words have the basic meaning of "understanding." In God's case, he has a full, complete, and total understanding of all things. God is the only one who could have given us knowledge. Any and all knowledge we have, must have come from him. This is why we refer to God as omniscient. The word omniscient comes from the Latin words *omni* meaning "all" and *science* meaning a "body of knowledge." God has all the knowledge we need in order to know who he is and how to live for his glory. When we were naturally sinful, however, God only gave us a limited amount of knowledge about him through General Revelation.

God's General Revelation

God began teaching us about himself through "general revelation" or "universal revelation." We call this knowledge general revelation because God gives it to all people, at all times in history, and in all places around the earth. The knowledge God gives to all people is that he exists and requires them to obey him. General revelation is available to all of us because it consists of two witnesses found in nature. The two witnesses are God's creation of the universe and God's providence in the world. Acts 14:16-17 says, "In past generations he allowed all the nations to walk in their own ways. Yet he did not leave himself without witness." These two natural witnesses are sufficient to prove to us that God exists *and* requires obedience from us. We may not immediately understand this last phrase, but it is important to realize that the natural witnesses reveal more than just that God exists. They reveal that God requires obedience from all people.[25]

God's Creation

The first natural witness is God's creation. Through the creation, God reveals to all people that he exists as a divine being with the eternal power to have created everything. Romans 1:19-21 says, "For what can be known about God is plain to them, because God has shown it to them. For his invisible attributes, namely, his eternal power and divine nature, have been clearly perceived, ever since the creation of the world, in the things that have been made. So they are without excuse [for not obeying God]." From the time God made people in the world, we all knew God existed because we saw his creation. Specifically, we realized he created us as his children, and he made the creation for us. When we look at the thousands of stars in the dark sky or gaze at the massive rock it took to form the mountains or stare into the depths of the ocean, we see that God made this for us. He did not make it and then decide to make us on the earth. He decided to make us long before he made the earth, and then he made the earth for us. God is similar to our parents who decide to have a child, and then go and prepare

---

[25] Because people know that God requires obedience, they also know that he will judge them for disobedience, and his judgment will be just.

everything for the child when he is born. God decided to make us, and then made everything in the universe for us.

Our existence and the existence of the creation for us reveals more than that God exists. It also reveals that God made all people for the purpose of obeying him and glorifying him. Nothing exists anywhere in the universe that God did not also make with a purpose. As insignificant as anything or anyone may appear to us, nothing is insignificant to God. God made every single thing that has ever existed anywhere in the universe with a purpose. This includes us on the earth. God made it evident to us that he exists as our creator, but he also made it evident to us that he created us for the purpose of glorifying him.

God's Provisions

The second natural witness is God's provisions to all people. Because all people are God's physical children, he provides them with all the things they need such as food, water, clothing, and shelter. Acts 14:17 says, "Yet he did not leave himself without witness, for he did good by giving you rains from heaven and fruitful seasons, satisfying your hearts with food and gladness." Like an earthly father, God provides all people, Christians as well as non-Christians, with the things that make them happy. God also provides all of them with the things that give them a higher quality of life such as good food, nice clothes, and beautiful homes. God's provisions to them extend throughout their entire lives so they always have the things they need, and even the things that make them happy. Sometimes we wonder what we would do if we lost our job, if our house burned down, or if our spouse died. God, however, like a father, takes care of us and provides for us. Even as God gives and takes from us throughout our lives, he always provides us with exactly what we need at different times in our lives. God's constant provisions to us serve as a consistent witness that he is our father and he cares for us. God's provisions to us also reveal to us that as his children we need to obey him and live how he wants.

Our Default Setting

God makes it evident to all people that he exists and they have to obey him. All people have this knowledge. No one can say that they do not know that God exists. No one can say that they did not realize they had to obey God. Even at the Judgment, no one can give God the excuse that they did not know that he existed and required obedience. Everyone is fully aware. Everyone knows. This knowledge forms the default setting of every person as it pertains to what they know about God. Every one of us, regardless of educational level, financial status, mental aptitude, and physical condition knows that God created us, and we have to obey him. This is why some of the prophets in the Scriptures such as Isaiah connected the creation of the world with the true God. Isaiah 42:5 says, "Thus says God, the Lord, who created the heavens and stretched them out, who spread out the earth and what comes from it." Every one of us who makes choices about right and wrong and who thinks about spiritual issues, knows that God exists as our creator and requires obedience from us. This is our default setting, and we cannot change it. As a result, we all need to know how to obey the one true God.

We Are All Religious

Because we all need to know how to obey God, every single one of us is religious or spiritual in some way. We all follow some kind of religion, even if it is not a formal one. A religion is simply a set of beliefs and practices about how we should live. Because we all want to know how to live, we are all religious. We as Christians follow the true religion[26] of Christianity, the religion of Jesus Christ. Non-Christians, however, follow one or more false religions. We can classify false religions into three broad categories; transcendent false religions, naturalistic false religions, and heathenistic false religions.

Transcendent False Religion

A transcendent false religion is a religion that includes a false god who *transcends* the material universe. A non-Christian may follow a transcendent false religion because of the various arguments[27] for a transcendent god's existence. These arguments include the cosmological,[28] the teleological,[29] and the moral[30] arguments. These arguments prove that the universe had a first cause, an intelligent designer, a moral law giver, respectively. Non-Christians connect these three entities to their own god, even though they actually pertain to the one true God. A Scriptural example of a transcendent false religion occurs in Acts 8:9-10 which says, "But there was a man named Simon, who had

---

[26] The difference between Christianity and non-Christian religions is not that one is a relationship and the others are religions. All religions involve a relationship between the god and the god's followers. The difference is Christianity is God-made, but other religions are all man-made.

[27] These arguments only provide evidence of a transcendent divine being, not a specific one. As such, even false religions that include a transcendent divine being use these arguments to prove their god exists.

[28] The cosmological argument asserts that in a series of causative actions, there must be a very first cause.

[29] The teleological argument asserts that there must be an intelligent designer of the universe.

[30] The moral argument asserts that because moral values exist, there must be a giver of those moral values.

previously practiced magic in the city...They all paid attention to him...saying, 'This man is the power of God that is great.'" The God in this passage is a transcendent false god who the people had mistakenly thought was the true God until they heard the gospel.

A non-Christian who follows a transcendent false religion responds to the natural witnesses by following the teachings of his transcendent false god. Because his god does not actually exist, he often follows his god's teachings through one or more middle-men who do actually exist or have existed. He calls these middle-men prophets or teachers. In following the teachings of his false god, he believes he is obeying the true God even though he is not. In order for us to know whether a religion is a transcendent false religion, we can ask, "In the religion, does the god exist outside of the material universe, and teach his followers how to live in some manner?"

Naturalistic False Religions

A naturalistic false religion is a religion in which there is a god who exists *within* the material universe. He exists within it because the material universe is all that exists.[31] The god may either be part of the material universe such as the sun. He may be the collective forces within the universe as a whole. In either case, the god exists within the material universe, not outside of it. While existing within the material universe, he interacts with his people in some way. The Scriptures give an example of a naturalistic religion in Ezekiel 8. Ezekiel 8:16 says, "About twenty-five men...worshiping the sun toward the east." In this passage, several Israelites had turned away from the true God and begun worshiping the sun.

A non-Christian who follows a naturalistic false religion responds to the natural witnesses by learning how the world functions. He uses his reasoning skills to analyze human nature, societal norms, and even the natural world systems themselves. Presuming he is part of the world, he applies this knowledge to his own life to learn how to live the right way within the world. He does not believe he needs faith, the mind of Christ, or the Holy Spirit to understand how to live the right way. In order for us to know whether a religion is a naturalistic false religion, we can ask, "In the religion, is the god part of the material world and its followers learn how to live the right way by analyzing how the world functions?"

---

[31] The view that the material world and the things within are all that exist is called materialism.

Heathenistic False Religions

A heathenistic false religion is a religion in which a non-Christian's god is essentially his own[32] passions and lusts that controls how he lives. God made each of us naturally sinful, but if God did not give us a new righteous spirit, we remain bound to our sin as non-Christians. A non-Christian's sin causes him to have certain passions and lusts that controls how he lives. Whatever is most pleasurable to him in different situations determines how he thinks, acts, and speaks. We can see an example of a heathenistic false religion in Philippians 3:18 which says, "For many...walk as enemies of the cross of Christ...their god is their belly." In this passage, these particular enemies of Christ are those who lived however they wish based on their appetites for food.

A non-Christian who follows a heathenistic false religion responds to the natural witnesses by denying in some way that the true God or any type of god exists. His god is his own passions so when he sees what God made clearly evident through the natural witnesses, he responds by denying that any kind of divine being exists and any kind of religion exists. Because of this, a non-Christian who follows a heathenistic false religion is sometimes an atheist[33] or an agnostic,[34] but not in every case. In order for us to know whether a religion is a heathenistic false religion, we can ask, "In the religion, does a follower follow his own passions and lusts, instead of a divine being of some kind?"

The Presence of the Natural Witnesses Cause Other Religions

The natural witnesses have always existed as long as we have. They cause all of us to be religious in some way and to some degree. This is our default setting, and there is nothing we can do to escape from this setting. Every person knows God exists. Every person knows he must obey God. Every person knows that he will be judged for how well he acts on his knowledge. As a result, every person either develops and/or follows some religion. At first, this sounds a little like God is at fault for the presence of other religions since he established the natural witnesses. God is not at fault as though he did

---

[32] The literal concept of heathen means, "one living on his own uncultivated land." The metaphorical concept of a heathen means, "One who does not follow any kind of formal religion, but does his own thing."

[33] Atheism affirmatively denies that the true God or any other false gods exist.

[34] Agnosticism passively denies that the true God or any other false gods exist by claiming we cannot know. Some have humorously said that an agnostic is an "atheist without guts." This is incorrect because agnosticism has nothing to do with courage or bravery.

something wrong. God, however, does establish false religions because of two factors working together.

The first factor is that God gives faith to those whom he chooses and withholds it from those whom he chooses. Romans 9:18 says, "So then he has mercy on whomever he wills, and he hardens whomever he wills." If the true God does not give us faith, we cannot know him or understand how to obey him. This is where the second factor comes into play. We still have the natural witnesses. The presence of the natural witnesses motivates all of us to respond to the fact that God exists and requires obedience. If non-Christians do not have faith, but have God's natural witnesses, they will follow either a transcendent false religion, a naturalistic false religion, a heathenistic false religion, or a combination of these.

However, the presence of false religions on the earth should not be unsettling for us. On the one hand, they exist and we live around many non-Christians who practice one, two, or all three of them. Whether a non-Christian follows a transcendent false religion, a naturalistic false religion, or a heathenistic false religion, he is still a non-Christian. One particular non-Christian is not any further from God than any other non-Christian.

On the other hand, God can give any non-Christian faith in Jesus Christ, if it is his will. Even if a non-Christian is a hard core believer and practitioner of a false religion, God can still give him faith in Christ. Even if a non-Christian stood before the true God and slandered him, God can still give him faith. If God does, a non-Christian will begin to know God and understand how to live for his glory. He will give up his false religion and begin following the religion of Christianity, the religion of the one true God.

Christianity

This was the case with us as Christians. For some of us, it brings tears to our eyes. Before God gave us faith, we followed a false god of some kind. We may not have known it, but we did. We gave our time, energy, and money to the religion of a false god. We did not know the one true God and had no desire to obey him for his glory. Even if someone were to present to us the most convincing arguments for glorifying the one true God, we still would not do it because living for God's glory would be repulsive to us. God, however, caused us to hear the gospel of Jesus Christ. We heard about Jesus' death and resurrection, and God gave us faith in Christ. When we received faith, we began to know God. He placed us as his people into his kingdom so that we would begin to follow his religion; Christianity.

The religion of God's kingdom is objective. We as Christians do not come up with how we can glorify God off the top of our heads. We do not reason and attempt to come up with ways to glorify God. Rather, we glorify God by obeying what God teaches us. God himself specifically and objectively gives us the knowledge about himself and how we should live in different situations and circumstances. When we follow this knowledge, we glorify God. The Scriptures call the knowledge about how to obey him in his kingdom the "truth."

The Truth

God's knowledge regarding the gospel of Jesus and how we should live in the kingdom of God is called the "truth." The English word truth is based on the Hebrew word *emeth* and the Greek word *aletheia*. Both of these words mean a body of knowledge from God pertaining to Jesus and how we should live in his kingdom. Some people may presume that the truth is simply knowledge that describes reality in general. For example, a person may say, "The sky is blue today." If this is the case, he considers it the truth. This understanding of the truth, however, pertains to how it is used in contemporary usage.

When the Scriptures use the word truth they use it more specifically. They use it to describe the knowledge pertaining to Jesus and the correct way to live in his kingdom for God's glory. For example, if someone were to say that we can receive a new regenerated spirit because of the death and resurrection of Jesus, this is the truth. It pertains to Jesus and how we can live for God's glory. The Scriptures reveal this understanding of the truth in John 18:37-38 which says, "I have come into the world - to bear witness to the truth. Everyone who is of the truth listens to my voice. Pilate said to him, 'What is truth?'" The truth that Jesus was speaking of was the gospel regarding himself and effectual theology for sound godly living in his kingdom. The Scriptures sometimes refer to the truth using various descriptors. Galatians 2:14 says, "The truth of the gospel." 2 Corinthians 11:10 says, "The truth of Christ" These and other passages describe that the truth pertains to Jesus.

Our having received the truth was directly dependent on God's giving us faith in Christ. When God gave us faith, we accepted the initial truth about the gospel of Jesus, and we spiritually died. God then gave us a new righteous spirit, the mind of Christ, and the Holy Spirit. The Holy Spirit began objectively teaching us the truth about Jesus and how to obey him so we could glorify God. John 16:13 says, "When the Spirit of truth comes, he will guide you into all the truth." The Scriptures explain the concept of

God giving us the truth and the concept of our accepting the truth through faith using the two analogies of light/darkness and sight/blindness. The Scriptures use these analogies in conjunction with each other in the following way.

The Analogies of Light/Darkness and Sight/Blindness

When God originally created the earth, he began placing naturally sinful people in it, but he did not give them the truth. When a person was born, he did not know God or how to live for his glory. His life was essentially an exhibition of sinfulness. We see this as we travel to various areas of the world. We see how people live and realize they do not naturally know how to live for God's glory. Proverbs 2:13 refers to how they live when it says, "Who forsake the paths of uprightness to walk in the ways of darkness." The natural state of the world from the time God made it to the present is metaphorically *dark*.

God, however, began teaching naturally sinful people in the world about who he is and how to live in his kingdom to glorify him. God did this through Jesus Christ who gives us the truth. When Jesus teaches us the truth of the gospel as well as the truth about how to live, he is metaphorically giving us the *light*. Jesus shines his light into the dark world by preaching the gospel to it and teaching it how to live. John 1:4-5 says, "In him was life, and the life was light of men. The light shines in the darkness, and the darkness has not overcome it." Jesus shined the light into the dark world through his Spirit prior to his incarnation. He himself shined the light as the Word of God when he was on the earth. After he left, he sent his Spirit to shine the light so we could know God through him and understand how to live.

As Jesus shined the light of the truth into the dark world, non-Christians could not understand it. God through Satan prevented them from understanding it by metaphorically *blinding* their eyes. 2 Corinthians 4:4 says, "The god of this world has blinded the minds of the unbelievers, to keep them from seeing the light of the gospel of [for] the glory of Christ." Non-Christians, even if they heard us explain the truth plainly and clearly to them, will not come to know and accept it on their own because Satan has blinded them.

God, however, gives certain non-Christians faith so they may accept the truth of the gospel and understand how to live[35] within God's kingdom for his glory. When God does this, he metaphorically gives them *sight* or *opens their eyes*. Acts 26:18 says, "To open their eyes, so that they may turn from darkness to light and from the power of Satan to God." When Acts 26:18 says, "to open their eyes," it is not referring to their eyelids being raised. It is referring to their eyes being able to receive light.[36] When God opens a non-Christian's eyes, he causes him to believe the truth of the gospel and accept the teachings of the Spirit so he may live, no longer within the dark world, but in the kingdom of God for God's glory.

We may have noticed with these analogies that the Scriptures equate the concept of metaphorically seeing with the concept of literally understanding. This makes perfect sense and should not seem unusual to us. We do this in our everyday lives. For example, if a math tutor explains a math problem to a student, he may say to him, "Do you see what I am saying?" This is equivalent to his saying, "Do you understand what I am saying?" The Scriptures sometimes do the same when they deal with the issue of understanding the truth.

God Gives Us More Truth

When God gave us faith in Jesus Christ, we began to understand the truth about him and how to live in his kingdom. John 8:12 says, "I am the light of the world; he who follows me will not walk in the darkness, but will have the light of life." In this verse the concept of following does not mean literally and physically following Jesus like the disciples did. It means we began following the truth that Holy Spirit gave us. The Holy Spirit began giving us the truth about God when he initially gave us faith in Christ. We understood who Christ was and what he did for us. We did not reason through and figure it out on our own.

The Holy Spirit then continued to give us more truth about Jesus and how to glorify him. He also gave us the necessary faith to accept this truth. The more truth the Holy Spirit gave us, the more faith he also gave us to accept it, and the better we began to

---

[35] Some people who practice the Hindu religion may place a red dot on their foreheads. This red dot functions as an eye and is sometimes called "the third eye." People may place this red dot or third eye on their foreheads to show others that they see or understand how to live. However, they can only truly understand how to live through the truth of Christ.

[36] A person is able to physically see because light enters his eyes.

know how to live for God's glory. The truth the Holy Spirit gave was not repulsive to us. We embraced it and had joy in obeying him because we glorified God. The Holy Spirit will continue to give us more and more truth until Christ finally returns. 1 Corinthians 13:12 says, "For now we see in a mirror dimly, but then face to face. Now, I know in part; then I shall know fully." When Jesus returns, something amazing happens. The Holy Spirit will give us a full amount of faith, and he will cause us to be fully illumined. All the truth there is to know about Jesus and how to glorify God, the Holy Spirit will instantly give us.[37] We will fully accept it and fully obey God.

We Can Fully Know God

When we hear the phrase "know fully" from 1 Corinthians 13:12, we may wonder if we can really know God fully. To rephrase the issue more intellectually, we may wonder if we as finite people with flesh and blood can fully know an infinite and magnificent God. The key to understanding this is to realize that our physical make-up is not related in any way to the amount of divine knowledge we can understand. It is not the size of our brains or even the level of our mental aptitude[38] that determines how much we can know about God. God determines how much we can know about himself. He reveals this knowledge through the Holy Spirit. John 16:13 says, "But when the Spirit of truth comes, he will guide you into all the truth, for he will not speak on his own authority, but whatever he hears he will speak."

The concept of our knowing God fully does not mean we will know absolutely everything about God. There are things we do not know about God and never will. These things belong to God alone. In the same way that each one of us knows things about ourselves that we will never tell another person, so does God. Deuteronomy 29:29 says, "The secret things belong to the Lord our God, but the things that are revealed belong to us and to our children forever." The concept of knowing God fully means we will have a full understanding of the things God wills to reveal to us. If God has not chosen to reveal certain knowledge to us, we will not receive it. In our case, God reveals to us Christ and how to live with him. At some point in the future, all of us as Christians will fully know Christ and how to live perfectly with him so we perfectly

---

[37] At this time, all church denominations will cease because every Christian will have all the truth.
[38] Spiritual knowledge is not dependent on a person's mental acumen, but rather faith. A person with a learning disability with greater faith knows more about God than a person with a high IQ with lesser faith.

glorify God. We will be in perfect union with Christ and knowing him is all we will need.

One of the things new employees need is training on how to apply the policies of their organization. They may have gone to a new employees' orientation and learned the policy, but they have not yet learned how to apply that policy in various situations and contexts. An employee's supervisor must come along side and train the employee to apply the organization's policy in his job. In a similar way, as we live in the kingdom of God, the Holy Spirit teaches us how to glorify God each moment of our lives in various situations and contexts. The Holy Spirit teaches us by giving us *wisdom*.

We Receive Wisdom

The truth about how God wants us to live in specific circumstances has a special name. It is called wisdom. The English word "wisdom" is based on the Hebrew word *chokmah* and the Greek word *sophia*. *Chokmah* and *sophia* in a basic sense mean "a body of coherently arranged knowledge pertaining to how we should live." God gives us wisdom through the Holy Spirit who he teaches us how to live in a particular situation so we glorify him. As we find ourselves in different contexts with different pressures, the Holy Spirit gives us godly wisdom so we know what to do. We need godly wisdom because every situation we are in is different, and therefore, the wisdom necessary to glorify God will be different. Proverbs 3:21-23 says, "Keep sound wisdom and discretion, and they will be life for your soul...Then you will walk on your way securely, and your foot will not stumble." The Scriptures refer to this kind of wisdom with different descriptors such as the "wisdom of God" in Ephesians 3:10 and "wisdom from above" in James 3:17.

There is a catch to this. The Scriptures predominantly refer to wisdom as knowledge from God about how we should live for his glory. However, in order to show that there is an opposing type of knowledge, the Scriptures mention a different kind of wisdom; one that comes from Satan. They call this type "wisdom of this world." 1 Corinthians 3:19 says, "For the wisdom of this world is folly with God." The wisdom of this world is knowledge about how we should live so that we please and glorify ourselves. Satan designs and gives worldly wisdom to both Christians as well as non-Christians through his demons through the medium of false doctrine. Satan tailors this doctrine so that it is pleasing to our sinful inclinations. As we find ourselves in various circumstances, such as what to say to someone or where to eat, Satan gives his wisdom to us so we glorify ourselves and ultimately sin. In addition to the phrase "wisdom of this world," the

Scriptures also refer to this kind of wisdom as "wisdom of men" in 1 Corinthians 2:5 and "earthly wisdom" in 2 Corinthians 1:12.

Knowledge about How to Live Comes from Christ

We live in a world where we seek knowledge of different kinds. We seek knowledge to understand how to grow plants, overcome diseases, and build decks on our houses. We need knowledge in order to live on this earth. There is one type of knowledge that is above all others…the knowledge about how to live in the kingdom of God so we glorify God. We can only obtain this knowledge from Jesus Christ. If we want to know how to do what is right and how to make good choices in our lives, we get this knowledge from Jesus Christ. If we want get up in the morning on a particular day, and live that day out exactly the way God wants, we get this knowledge from Jesus Christ. Jesus himself will give us this knowledge through the Holy Spirit in the form of godly wisdom. When we listen to him and obey him, we can glorify God. 3 John 4 says, "I have no greater joy than to hear that my children are walking in the truth."

Chapter 6

Why God Limits Our Ability to Glorify Him

We often hear about successful people such as professional athletes or movie stars and wonder how they became successful. We may read their biographies or watch television shows detailing their lives to learn how they lived so we might emulate them in some way. Some of us, however, may not realize that behind every successful person is the one true God who controls their lives. A successful person may have indeed worked hard, and he may have sacrificed earthly comforts and pleasures. He may have done many things to be successful, but none of them actually made him successful. He became successful because God specifically controlled his life so he would be.

This principle is also true for us as Christians. As we look at our lives, we realize that we were born sinfully, but became righteous and began living for God's glory. Most of us can give some kind of testimony to this change in our lives. However, we may not fully realize that behind this change was God himself. We did not cause ourselves to become righteous so we could glorify God. God did. This may go against popular wisdom that says we have the power within ourselves to choose what we do, what we think, what we make of our lives. This popular wisdom is not correct. If we think about it long enough, we realize it cannot be correct because we cannot get the power from within ourselves to do anything. We get the power and ability to glorify God from God himself because he is power and controls our lives.

God Is Power

God causes us to glorify him because God is power. The word power is based on the Hebrew word *koach* and the Greek word *dunamis*. *Koach* and *dunamis* mean strength, ability, or force. God is the sole power or force in the entire universe that causes all things to happen. He was the sole power that caused all things to come into being when he commanded them to. He is also the sole power that makes all things happen anywhere in the universe at any given moment. Every planet revolving around the sun receives its power from God. Every fish swimming deep underneath the Arctic ice receives its power from God. Because of this, we sometimes refer to God as omnipotent. The word omnipotent comes from the Latin words *omni* meaning "all" and *potent* meaning "power." Because God is omnipotent, he has absolute control over everything within the creation. He controls everything about us and the universe he made for us. Acts 17:28 testifies to this when it says, "In [Through] him we live and move and have our being."

God Controls Our Lives

As we think about the concept of God's absolute control, it can be very complex to our minds. We may see a leaf blowing across the lawn and wonder if God controls that leaf. If God truly is omnipotent, then he does. Some of us though may not apply God's omnipotence to leaves. We apply it to events such as God's control of the earth moving around the sun, but not so much to leaves blowing across lawns. God, however, does control minor events such as this, and we refer to him as being "immanent." The word immanent comes from the Latin words *in* and *manere*, and means "to remain in." The word immanent does not mean God is part of the world such as a tree or mountain. The word immanent also does not mean God physically lives in the world like we do. Rather, God is immanent because he is operative in the world and controls everything in it.

The analogy of a model railroad may help us understand the concept of God's immanence a little better. Some people have designed a model railroad layout in their homes. They have laid out every piece of the train track, building, tree, and finally the train itself in the layout. They placed everything in it based on where they wanted it and how they wanted the layout to function. They have also hooked up the power supply and knew exactly how to maneuver the train at their will. These individuals were immanent within that railroad layout. They did not live within the layout nor were they physically part of it. Rather, they operated it and controlled it exactly how they wanted. In a similar, but greater way, the omnipotent God is immanent in our lives and in the world he made for us. He is operative within it and controls it exactly how he wants. Even a leaf that falls to the ground and blows across our lawn, God controls.

For us to understand that God is immanent in the world requires more than just saying it. We need to see and understand the ways in which he is. The omnipotent God is immanent in the world and controls our lives in four ways:

1. God Controls the Inherent Nature of Every Object

God controls the inherent nature of every object within the universe. God created every object of certain basic elements. Many if not all of these elements are listed in the periodic table of elements which we learned about in school. God made these elements to be the building blocks and the structural foundation of every object in the entire universe. God also made these elements to never change, at least in the current age. Psalm 104:5 says, "He set the earth on its foundations, so that it should never be moved." All objects in the universe may have different forms with different names, but underneath their various forms are these elements which make them up. God made every literal thing anywhere in the universe at any time in history to be made up of these elements. A rock lying on the surface of Mars and the cereal we ate for breakfast are all made up of these elements.

Because God made every object to be made up of these elements, he controls how they interact with one another. We call these various interactions the laws of nature. The laws of nature are simply a way to explain how God causes various objects to interact with each other. The laws of nature will never change, unless God causes them to. For example, oil and water will never mix, and cedar will always smell like cedar. God created the laws of nature, and he controls how every object in the universe interacts with one another. The wind blows at certain times, at certain speeds, and in certain directions because God controls it. We ourselves may control various objects in the world such as the speed of our cars. However, our control is relative and based on how God controls all objects.

As God controls objects, he does not always follow his own laws of nature. God normally[39] follows his natural laws, but occasionally throughout history, he has overridden them in order to show that he is in control. For example, in 2 Kings 6:5-7, God's prophets under Elisha's leadership were building houses in order to conduct God's ministry. As they were cutting down trees, an axe head came off of its axe and sank into a river. The prophet Elisha, through the power of God, made the axe head float. God overrode his natural laws as a sign that he was establishing a place for the prophets to minister in order to return Israel to faithfulness. God normally uses his

---

[39] The difference between supernatural laws and natural laws is simply normality. God normally uses natural laws, but can use supernatural ones if he chooses because he can do whatever he wants, whenever he wants, wherever he wants.

natural laws to control objects, but he can and may override them in order to specifically show he is control.[40]

God controls the inherent nature of all objects because he designed them. This includes us. We cannot breathe naturally underwater, and contrary to some opinions we cannot go back in time. Things such as these belong to the world of fantasy, not reality. The reality is that God designed us in a certain way in this world to glorify him. He then controls us so that we do. God's control over us is much more than control over what our bodies can do. God also controls us by giving us our interests.

2. God Controls Our Interests

Each of us has various interests because of how God inherently made us. God made each of us with a body. God made each of our bodies by causing us to have certain parents who passed on their genes to us. We look, walk, and talk a certain way because of how God made our bodies. God also made each of us with a spirit. God made each of our spirts in the likeness of our parents so we each have a certain nature. We think, speak, and act similar to our parents because God made our spirits to be like their spirits. Then when we were born, God caused our parents to raise and nurture each of us in certain ways. God made some of us to grow up in Christian homes while he caused others of us to grow up in non-Christian homes. He gave some of us strict parents while he gave others of us lenient parents. God caused each of us to be raised and nurtured in a certain way.

As a result of how God made us, we each have certain interests. They are part of who we are. We have interests such as eating certain foods, visiting certain places, and wearing certain styles of clothing, among hundreds of others. We cannot change our interests because they are inherent to how God made us. Only God can change our interests because he gave them to us. Furthermore, we live each moment of our lives attempting to have our various interests met. If we think about it, though, we have many, many interests. It would seem impossible for us to have all of our many interests met. It is not impossible, however. It is quite the opposite because God also designed us to fulfill our many interests by prioritizing them.

God designed us so that we prioritize all of our interests in descending order and always seek our greatest self-interest at any given moment. We give the more important

---

[40] We usually term these types of acts supernatural. In addition to natural and supernatural, there is a third category called preternatural. Preternatural pertains to heightened natural abilities such as with Superman. Preternatural laws, however, do not actually exist.

interests a higher priority and lesser important interests a lower priority. We then seek to fulfill them based on how we prioritized them. We move down our list of interests and always choose to pursue a greater interest before a lesser interest. In each micro-moment of time, we prioritize our interests and seek to fulfill our greatest interest. Psalm 37:23 says, "The steps of a man are established by the Lord."

We can see this through the analogy of our walking someplace. We will go to many places throughout our lives because we have an interest in doing so. Each time we go to a particular place, our going there becomes our primary interest. We will then walk there using the most direct route. The only time we deviate from the most direct route is when a lesser interest temporarily takes priority over a higher interest in going to that particular place. For example, if we live in a major city, we may have an interest in walking to the local grocery store. This becomes our primary interest, and we will walk there using the most direct route. However, we may have a lesser interest that temporarily takes priority such as when we walk around a puddle. However, unless there is a lesser interest that takes priority, we will always take what we consider to be the most direct route in going to that place because that is our greatest interest.

God designed each of us spiritually and bodily, and gave each of us all of our interests. He also designed us to choose our greatest self-interest at any given time. Because of this, God determines every single choice we make. We do not arbitrarily or randomly choose to have certain interests, and we cannot change which interest to fulfill. God, however, does. He is the one who determines which choice we make. Proverbs 16:9 says, "The heart of man plans his way, but the Lord establishes his steps." We may dream about what we want to do, but we are bound to follow our interests because God gave them to us and determines how we follow them.[41]

Why We Need to Make Choices

We may wonder why we even need to make choices at all since God seems to have predetermined what choices we make. We may wonder why we cannot just sit back and do nothing. Simply put, we do not sit back and do nothing because we cannot. In addition to God designing us to have our interests, he also designed us to make moment to moment choices about how we have all of our interests fulfilled. We cannot change how God designed us. We cannot sit back and not make a choice. In other words, we

---

[41] The person or thing that determines our choices is called the "antecedent cause." The view that God is the antecedent cause is called Determinism, and it is the correct view. The view that we are our own antecedent cause is called Self-Determinism, and it is a false view.

cannot choose not to choose. God made us to always choose what is in our greatest self-interest in each moment of our lives, even if it is to question how we make choices.

Because God made us in such a way that we have to make choices, he informs us of certain information so we can make certain choices. He uses individuals to do this, and he even uses our own memory. He uses things such as these to teach and inform us so that we can make the choices he determined that we will make. For example, if a boy is lost in the woods, but God determined that he find his way out, God will use someone or something else to inform the boy so that he finds his way out. He may use the boy's memory of something, or he may send someone to find the boy, or he may withhold both so that the boy keeps walking and eventually comes to a road. God causes us to make certain choices by influencing us in such a way so we will make the choices he determines we make.

Because God controls our choices, he also controls everything about each of our lives. Everything about our lives is the result of the choices we have made, choices our parents made, or choices hundreds of other people made. The result of all of this is that we each have different assignments in life, and God therefore controls each assignment.

3. God Controls Our Assignments

God gave each one of us our interests, and they are different than anyone else's. As we grew up, we pursued our interests and made different choices about how to live each day. We made choices about what foods to eat, what clothes to wear, what friends to have, among others. When we became adults, we made choices about where to live for different purposes and who to live with. Some of us are single, live in an urban environment, and enjoy riding a bike. Some of us are married, live in a rural environment, and like to travel to foreign countries. Every one of us is different because God made each of us to have different interests than anyone else.

Because of the way God physically made us and the interests he gave us, he assigns to us the various aspects of our lives. One such aspect is the various places we will live during our lives. God has determined the places we will live, and when we will live there throughout our lives because how he inherently made us. Acts 17:26 says, "He made from one man every nation of mankind to live on all the face of the earth, having determined allotted periods and the boundaries of their dwelling place." We may think we can live anywhere we want, but we will only live in a certain place if we have an interest in living there. For example, a man may live in Boston because he took a job there. He took a job in Boston because God determined that he would by causing him to be inherently made and have interests to take a job in Boston. God did not force him to take a job in Boston. Furthermore, the person did not freely choose to take a job in Boston. Rather, he chose to take a job in Boston because of the way God inherently made him and the interests God gave him.

This may sound deep, but it is only one aspect of the many aspects that God determines. God also determines the day we will die. God has determined the day we die because of how he inherently made us and the interests he gave us. Job 14:5 says, "Since his days are determined, and the number of his months is with you, and you have appointed his limits that he cannot pass." For example, suppose a man dies of a heart attack on a certain day at a certain time because he observed poor eating habits throughout his life. God determined that he would die on that day at that time by causing him to be inherently made and have interests conducive to poor eating habits that would eventually cause him to die on that day at that time. This may not seem very acceptable to some people, but God worked like this so he would be glorified. He is glorified by our sinning against him and receiving in our bodies the result of our sin.

Some of us may have qualms about the role God has in our choices and the lack of a role we have. We may think, on the one hand, that God does not have this much control. On the other hand, we think we have much more. Regardless, one thing most of us do believe is that God made our spirits. We obviously did not make our own spirits. Our parents did not make our spirits. Our spirits did not just appear in our bodies. God made each of our spirits, and because he did, he controls each of our spiritual conditions.

4. God Controls Our Spiritual Conditions

God created each of us with a naturally sinful spirit and body. When we were born, we each had sin within us. Psalm 51:5 says, "I was brought forth in [with] iniquity, and in [with] sin did my mother conceive me." The sin within us caused us to have interests in obtaining things for ourselves that brought us glory and pleasure. Sin caused us to want tangible things such as an expensive home that we could show off. Sin also caused us to want intangible things such as a position of power so we could dominate others. Sin caused us to want things so we pleased and glorified ourselves instead of God. We lived our entire lives seeking sinful types of things for our own glory and pleasure.

God, however, caused some of us to receive faith in Jesus Christ. Having received faith, we followed Christ in the likeness of his death and resurrection. God transformed us by freeing us from sin and making us righteous in Christ's likeness. He placed us in the kingdom of God as righteous people freed from sin. As members of the kingdom of God, we no longer desired to glorify ourselves and pursue sinful interests. Instead, we pursued godly interests as Christ did that pleased and glorified God. We wanted homes that God gave us based on how he wanted us to live. We wanted a job that God gave us so we could serve him. God gave us faith so that we began to want things that brought glory to God instead of ourselves. God gave faith to us because he controls us. His giving us faith completely altered our lives, not only in eternity, but here on this earth in the present age. We live to glorify God here and now in the kingdom of God.

God Must Be in Control

Given all the ways God controls us and the world we live in, he must be omnipotent. He controls the inherent nature of every object including us. He controls each of our interests so we always choose as he determines. He controls each of our assignments in life so we are never left on our own. He controls each of our spiritual conditions by giving us or keeping us from having faith in Christ. God is certainly omnipotent. God exercises his omnipotence in the world and in our lives so his glory is revealed in the world. If God did not or could control everything, he could not cause his glory to be displayed because he would not have control over it.

This understanding of God's control is somewhat restrictive, at least for us. It makes God look like he is a marionettist, and we are simply the marionettes dangling in the air. This analogy captures the thoughts of many people including some of us as Christians. We may be reluctant to accept the absolute control of God in the world and in our lives. However, it is absolutely true! God is indeed omnipotent and controls everything including us for his own glory. If we ever doubt the level of control God has, consider Amos 4:7-13 which says, "I would send rain on one city, and send no rain on another city…I sent among you pestilence after the manner of Egypt; I killed your young men with the sword. For behold, he who forms the mountains and creates the wind, and declares to man what is his thought…the Lord, the God of hosts, is his name!"

On the other end of the omnipotence spectrum, there are people who deny the existence of God, and as a corollary, any level of control he may have. However, these people are certainly not unintelligent or ignorant of basic logic. They have been living in the world long enough to understand basic ideas pertaining to cause and effect and absolute control. They know something must be in control. There has to be. Nothing occurs randomly. It is logically and practically impossible for anything in the created order to be free[42] and outside of transcendent control. Knowing this, they believe something must be in control. They usually called this thing "fate."

The Concept of Fate

Some non-Christians believe in the concept called fate that they presume controls the universe and especially their lives. They believe fate is the power which controlled everything in such a way that they were born in a particular city at a particular time in history. Fate caused them to go a particular school and meet their spouse. Fate caused them to have a certain number children who continued the circle of life. Some of us as Christians may believe in or at least entertain the concept of fate because it is a dominant view among many non-Christians.

The truth is, fate does not exist, and certainly does not control anything. Non-Christians only believe in fate because of the absence of the truth about God. We as Christians have faith, as well as the Holy Spirit within us who will teach us the truth about God and his absolute control. When he does, we can accept it, and our lifestyles will reflect our acceptance of this truth. For example, we will be able to pray sincere prayers which are answered. They will be answered because they will be based on faith in God who actually exists and controls everything. If we did not have faith that God was in total control, we would not have a good reason to pray. Any prayer we offered would not be sincere because we would be praying to someone who we did not believe was in total[43] control, and therefore, was not in a position to change anything. With faith, however, we do know that God controls absolutely everything.

The fact that God controls everything brings about a burning question in our minds and hearts, a question we must have answered. "If God in is control, why do bad things happen to us?"

Why Bad Things Happen to Us

This may be a common question for some people, but it is a little too vague, at least the word *bad* is. It is more appropriate to ask, "Why does God who has absolute control cause people to experience pain and suffering?" God's purpose for creating everything

---

[42] God is and always will be the only free being. A free being and God are one and the same. If we think we are free, it is tantamount to thinking we are God.
[43] If there is any entity anywhere in the universe that God does not have control over, then God does not have absolute control. However, if we think about it long enough, we soon realize he would not have any control. God's control in the universe is an all-or-nothing principle.

is to bring glory to himself. God did not bring everything into existence because he was bored. He certainly did not do it to exercise malicious control over people. God made everything to display the highest and most magnificent glory there is; i.e. his own.

God displays his glory by first making us sinful. This may seem strange to us, but it is not strange to a perfect God. He knows exactly why he did this. Everyone in the world sins and fails to display God's glory. When we sin, we may think we have a right to sin, but we do not. No one has a right to sin. Adversely, God has a right to be glorified. Given this juxtaposition, God also has a right to cause sinful people in the world to experience pain and suffering of various kinds for sinning and not glorifying him. For this reason, when we experience a painful situation, we internally ask, "What did I do?" Even when a judge must decide a punishment for a criminal, he wants to do it based on the seriousness of the crime. The painful situation he imposes must match the crime. Each of us knows God has a right to cause people to experience pain and suffering because of their sin.

When God causes us to experience pain and suffering, it motivates us to acknowledge our own sinfulness and respond. Sometimes we may experience a personal tragedy, such having marriage problems. These motivate us personally to examine our lives for sin, and respond by turning away from it. At other times, we may experience a common tragedy, such as destruction of personal property caused by a tornado. It motivates all the people involved to examine their lives for sin, and respond by turning away from it. This is similar to when parents discipline a child for doing something wrong. The parents cause the child to experience pain and suffering so the child thinks about his sin and responds by turning away from it.

Things are a little different with non-Christians though. When God causes non-Christians to experience pain and suffering, they do not respond at all to God. They do not know God, and they do not believe he is the one causing the pain and suffering. All they know is that they are going through discomfort, and they want it to stop. If they do respond, they will only do so in order to avoid the pain and suffering. In essence, they do not respond to God, but to the pain and suffering. It is like a child who is disciplined by someone he does not know. The child does not perceive that the discipline is in fact discipline. He perceives it as malice because he does not know who is doing it or why. He only responds by trying to avoid the pain and suffering.

When God, however, causes us to experience pain and suffering, we respond to God because we know him. We know that he loves us, and we love him in return. We know he is the one doing it, and we may say things such as, "God is control." We also respond, not to the pain and suffering, but to God. Our pain and suffering serves as motivation for us to turn from sin, and we do. We may begin obeying God in a certain way, which we did not do before. For this reason, Romans 8:28 says, "And we know that for those who love God all things work together for good, for those who are called according to his purpose." The word *good* in this passage refers to God's glory. It means God causes all things in our lives even pain and suffering so he is glorified, and it is good, very good.

God Empowers Us to Glorify God through Jesus Christ

When we take a moment to think about God, we realize God must control our lives. He must be omnipotent. The laws of nature teach it. Logic demands it. Most importantly, the Scriptures proclaim it. God created everything to be absolutely dependent on him including us. He created us to need a controller to direct us toward fulfilling the purpose for which he made us, i.e. his glory. For this reason, God is sovereign, and controls us through Jesus Christ as his Sovereign.

Jesus as God's Sovereign has exclusive control over all things, including and especially us, in order for God's glory to be reflected. 1 Timothy 6:15 says, "He [Jesus Christ] who is the blessed and only Sovereign, the King of Kings and Lord of Lords." The concept of sovereignty means a king or a comparable person has exclusive control over his jurisdiction so his purpose is carried out and his will is fulfilled. God created us for the purpose of reflecting his glory. We can fulfill our purpose because God transformed us from being naturally sinful to being righteous. He then placed us in the kingdom of God where Jesus Christ is the sovereign ruler over us. Colossians 1:16 says, "For by him all things were created, in heaven and on earth, visible and invisible, whether thrones or dominions or rulers or authorities - all things were created through him and for him."

Some of us have written down goals that we wanted to accomplish in our lives. Some of them pertain to a place we wanted to visit or a skill we wanted to learn. Our accomplishing any goals whether large or small is dependent on God and his will for our lives. Some goals we may meet, but others we may not. It is up to God because he made us and controls our lives. For us, the most important thing God wants is for us to live for his glory. This is his purpose for creating us. God empowers us to fulfill this purpose through Jesus, the Sovereign ruler over all things. Jesus exercises his authority over our lives so we can glorify God. Jesus continues to do this even to the end of the age. When everything in the current age is completed and passed away, we will glorify God perfectly. This will happen not because we did so on our own, but because the omnipotent God was immanently involved in our lives. At the end of all things, there will be at least three absolutes. Jesus is king over his kingdom on the earth. We live in his kingdom as his people. He rules over us so we can glorify God without hindrance.

Chapter 7

Who Jesus Would Be and What He Would Establish

When movies sometimes begin, everything is normal, and everyone is happy, but then a problem arises. The problem might be a man-made disturbance, or it might be a natural disaster. Whatever the problem, it can only be rectified in one way and only by one man. This man becomes the hero. This basic plot line is not uncommon in movies. It is also pertinent to God. God created us to glorify him, and this is our purpose for living. God, however, also made each of us to be naturally sinful. From the time we were born we could not glorify him. This is our problem, and it is a big problem. Not only that, but there is one and only one person who can rectify our problem. This is where the hero enters. His name is Jesus.

Jesus Is the Son of God

As Christians, we have heard of Jesus. When we think about him, we usually think about his life while on Earth during his first coming. However, long before his birth, and even before God had created the universe, Jesus existed. We may not realize how a man born on the physical earth at a certain time in earthly history could have existed before God created it, but he did. Prior to the creation, Jesus existed in Heaven with God the Father as a spirit only. Jesus as a spirit existed with God the Father as well as the Holy Spirit. They all dwelt together and interacted with each other because there was nothing else that existed. God had not yet created angels, Satan, demons, or even the universe.

As the only entities who existed, God the Father, Jesus, and the Holy Spirit were all divine. No one of the three was more or less divine than the other two. There was no degree of divinity that existed. There was no such thing as mostly divine or even partly divine. All three forms of God were fully and equally divine. To understand this concept a little better, we can look at the analogy of a family. Families have members such as fathers, mothers, sons, and daughters. Each family member is equal in the sense that they are all part of the family. They all live in the same house, share the same rooms, and use the same appliances. No one is more of a family member than another, and no one is less of a family member than another. This is similar to Jesus. God the Father, Jesus, and the Holy Spirit are all equally divine. No one of them is more or less divine than the others.

It is important to realize that equality in essence is different than equality in position. We may have noticed this as we thought about the above analogy in light of our own families. Everyone in our families is equally part of the family, but those within it are not equal in position. Fathers have the highest authority, then mothers, then children based on age. Very few of us would tell our fathers that we are equal to them in position, without them replying in a way that we would not soon forget. Though Jesus was equal in essence to God the Father and the Holy Spirit, these three were not equal in authority. Within their relationship together, there existed a hierarchy. God the Father had the highest authority over all things. No one has more authority than God the Father had or has; not at any time or in any place throughout all eternity. Jesus as a spirit, however, had the second highest authority. God the Father gave Jesus his authority and sent him to Earth to do his work. John 12:49 says, "For I have not spoken on my own authority, but the Father who sent me has himself given me a commandment – what to say and what to speak."

Because of this relationship, Jesus is God the Father's son. He is of the same essence as God the Father, but subordinate to him, just like we are subordinate to our fathers. As a son, Jesus performed work on behalf of his Father. One of the first things Jesus did was to create everything. Some of us may have thought God the Father created everything. He did, but he did not do it alone. He did it through Jesus.

Jesus Was the Agent of Creation

God the Father created everything through Jesus his son as the agent of the creation. When the Scriptures use the phrase, "And God said, 'Let there be light'" such as in Genesis 1:3, God in this verse is not a reference to God the Father alone. The word God in this verse is the title *Elohim*, and it includes the spirit of Jesus. Even though God the Father was the source from which everything came, Jesus was the agent who created it. This is why Colossians 1:16 says regarding Jesus and the creation, "For by him [the spirit of Jesus] all things were created…all things were created through him and for him."

We can see that Jesus was the agent of the creation in Matthew 14. In this passage, Jesus along with his disciples fed five thousand people. After the people ate, Jesus had his disciples get into a boat to sail across the sea. Jesus himself, however, went to a mountain to pray. Later in the evening, the wind became strong over the water of the sea, and it caused the disciples to have trouble as they went. During the night, Jesus came to them walking on the water. When Peter saw Jesus, Jesus enabled him to walk on the water as well. However, when Peter saw the wind, he began to sink. Jesus took hold of Peter, and the two of them got into the boat. Jesus then caused the wind to die down. We may have heard this story so many times over the years that we just accept it as normal, but it was far from normal. People do not just walk on top of water, and enable others to do so. They certainly cannot command the wind to die down, and it obeys. The disciples knew this, and it was the reason they called Jesus the "Son of God." Matthew 14:25-33 says, "And in the fourth watch of the night he [Jesus] came to them, walking on the sea…those in the boat worshiped him saying, 'Truly, you are the Son of God.'" The disciples did not arbitrarily call Jesus the Son of God. They specifically called him the Son of God because they recognized Jesus as God who was the agent of the creation, and who had authority over it.

When Jesus created the world, he created it to contain sinful people. He did not create it to contain perfect, righteous, or sinless people. He created it so that sinful people would inhabit it, and he would eventually destroy them because of their sin. Because of this, Jesus did not initially rule over the world. Jesus certainly made the world, and he certainly has authority as the divine agent of the creation. However, Jesus created Satan, and God gave him the authority to rule over the world of sinful people. Satan's rule, however, would only be temporary.

Jesus Did Not Initially Rule

Jesus created Satan as a spirit to begin ruling the world in such a way as to entice people to sin and glorify themselves. This was perfectly in line with God's plan for the world. God did not create Satan as an afterthought to making the world. God did not create Satan by accident. God created him as a spirit to specifically rule over a world containing sinful people beginning with Adam and Eve. For this reason, John 12:31 refers to Satan as, "The ruler of this world." Satan rules over the world in such a way to prevent the people of the world from obeying God, which is the opposite of what Jesus will do. Throughout history, these people formed nations, countries, and other types of populaces, all of which are distinct based on the level of rule Satan has over them. Satan's rule is temporary, however, and he will not always rule. At a time in the future, Satan will rule over one final nation on Earth, but Jesus will destroy him, and the nation he rules. Prior to Jesus doing this, he will begin to establish his kingdom where he rules. This kingdom will be called the "kingdom of God."

The Kingdom of God

We do not normally hear the word kingdom, unless we are reading the Scriptures or learning about history. So, we may not know exactly what a kingdom is. A kingdom contained a king and the people he ruled. Wherever the king and his people were, that is where the kingdom was. The king established laws for his people to uphold. In return, the people showed allegiance to the king and obeyed his laws.

The kingdom of God is a kingdom not unlike any other kingdom. In the kingdom of God, though, Jesus rules over us as Christians so we obey him and display the qualities of life, knowledge, power, and righteousness. The result of Jesus' rule over us and our display of these qualities will be God's glory. 1 Thessalonians 2:12 says, "We exhorted each one of you and encouraged you and charged you to walk in a manner worthy of God, who calls you into his own kingdom and glory." We will glorify God with the glory he most assuredly deserves and which he did not receive from the world.

God began building the kingdom of God by providing those in the sinful world with information about it. Naturally sinful people did not know anything about a kingdom of God. They looked around the world they lived in and there was nothing to indicate that God was establishing a kingdom of righteous people. As such, God began providing information to people about this kingdom. This was similar to a billboard. As people move into a city and drive around, they may not know anything about the businesses and organizations within the city. Billboards, however, provide them with good information. If they have a need for a certain business and see one advertised on a billboard, they can use this information. When God began building the kingdom of God, he gave people information about it by speaking through Jesus in what God referred to as the "Word of God."

The Word of God

All throughout the Scriptures God, through Jesus and the Holy Spirit, spoke to people in many different ways and for many different purposes. In many of those instances, God gave the "Word of God" or the "Word of the Lord." The word "word" in the phrase "Word of God" is based on the Hebrew word *debar* and the Greek word *logos*. Both words mean "speech which leads." When God gave the "Word of God," he was leading people to repent and begin obeying him. Jeremiah 13:8 says, "Then the word of the Lord came to me: Thus says the Lord…This evil people, who refuse to hear my words, who stubbornly follow their own heart." God's word often consisted of commands to people to obey him along with either promises of blessing or curses based on how they responded. For this reason, God's Word was divisive because it caused people to choose between two kingdoms. People had to decide to continue sinning in line with the kingdom of this world ruled by Satan, or they had to decide to repent of their sin in line with the kingdom of God. Because of the decisive nature of God's word, God was leading people to respond to him.

How Jesus Gave the Word of God

Jesus through the Holy Spirit began giving the Word of God immediately after he had created the livable earth. We refer to this first time as the *protoevangelium* meaning "the first proclamation of the gospel." The *protoevangelium* involved Jesus through the Spirit giving the first command to Adam and Eve so they would respond to him. After they responded by disobeying the Word of God, the Spirit spoke to them about their corresponding punishments. The Spirit then turned and spoke to Satan as well because he was the current ruler of the world and was involved with Adam and Eve's disobedience to the Word of God. When Jesus through the Spirit spoke to Satan, he promised enmity between his own followers and Satan's children. This enmity would ultimately end when Jesus destroyed Satan along with his children and replaced him as ruler of the kingdom of God.

When Jesus initially spoke to Satan about the kingdom of God, the kingdom would not come for hundreds of years in the future, but it would still come. It would come when Jesus came, and his people could enter it at that time. Because of this, God continued to give his word to various people throughout all of history so they could enter the coming kingdom. It was like the owner of a baseball team announcing the team's schedule intermittently throughout the season. People can learn when the games are and attend if they wish. Jesus gave his word throughout history so his people could turn to him and enter his kingdom when it arrived with him. Even if one of God's people were dead when Jesus came, they could still enter it because entering the kingdom of God was not about physically entering it. We entered the kingdom of God when the Holy Spirit cleansed and regenerated our spirits. John 3:5 says, "Truly, truly,

I say to you, unless one is born of water and the Spirit, he cannot enter the kingdom of God."

As such, prior to Jesus' incarnation, he continued giving the Word of God as he existed as a spirit in Heaven. Jesus, however, did not speak directly to people like we speak to each other. If one of us speaks to another, we simply begin talking to each other face to face. Prior to Jesus' incarnation, this was not how Jesus spoke to people when he gave his word. Jesus used certain individuals to transmit the Word of God to the people he intended to receive it. This was not unlike the president of a certain country transmitting a message to one of the citizens of the country. He usually did not do it directly, but rather used certain individuals to do it.

Jesus to the Holy Spirit to Angels

When Jesus intended to give his word to a particular recipient, he first gave it to the Holy Spirit. The Holy Spirit in turn gave it to an angel so that all of those who had the message were in Heaven. The angels alone then went to Earth and spoke with Jesus' intended recipients. Hebrews 2:2 says, "For since the message declared by angels." God's angels were spirit in form so in order for them to speak to a physical recipient of God's Word on Earth, they needed assume some kind of physical, earthly form. They did this by taking the form of an entire man, part of a man such as his voice or his hand, an animal, a plant, or other similar thing.

Angels to Jesus' Intended Recipients

When an angel took one of these earthly forms, he gave God's Word by either speaking or writing the message in a language that the intended recipients could understand. We can never know what these languages were, however, because we do not have any records indicating the language of the original communication. When an angel communicated to Jesus' intended recipients in whatever form and through whatever language, he may have appeared to the intended recipient in several different ways. An angel may have appeared his intended recipient in real time such as with Moses and the burning bush. He may have also appeared to his intended recipient in a dream while he was asleep such as with Joseph when the angel told him to take Mary as a wife. Lastly, an angel may have appeared to Jesus' intended recipient in a vison while he was awake such as with John when he received the vision within the book of Revelation. Angels may have taken one of several means to give Jesus' intended recipients his word, but in each, Jesus gave his word, and his intended recipients received it.

Angels to a Prophet First

This may seem to us like a complex way in which to give a message, but it is not complex to God. God gave his word in different ways, through different individuals because of all the various circumstances that people were in and his will for how they would receive his word. Now, the various means in which God gave his word gets even more complex. Angels did not always speak directly to Jesus' intended recipients. Sometimes an angel would speak to a prophet first who would in turn speak with Jesus' intended recipients. 2 Peter 1:20 says, "No prophecy of Scripture comes from someone's own interpretation…but men [prophets] spoke from God as they were carried along by the Holy Spirit." So whether an angel himself or a prophet gave the Word of God, Jesus had given his word, and the people had received it.

Jesus Was the Word

In the course of time, Jesus came to Earth. When he did, he was called, "the Word" because he had been the one giving his word through the Holy Spirit to people before his incarnation. In other words, he was called the Word after he incarnated himself because he had been the one giving God's Word in his pre-incarnate state. John 1:1 says, "In the beginning was the Word, and the Word was with God, and the Word was God. He was in the beginning with God." Like we may have suspected, Jesus as the Word did not cease giving the Word of God while on Earth. Jesus in his incarnated state spoke to his intended recipients in the same way he had done in his pre-incarnate state. Hebrews 1:1-2 says, "Long ago, at many times and many ways, God spoke to our fathers by the prophets, but in these last days he has spoken to us by his Son."

When Jesus began his ministry, he preached that the kingdom of God had arrived in him. Mark 1:14 says, "Now after John was arrested, Jesus came into Galilee, proclaiming the gospel of God, and saying, 'The time is fulfilled, and the kingdom of God is at hand; repent and believe in the gospel.' The incarnated Jesus called people to repentance and obedience in line with the Kingdom of God. However, for them to repent and obey, Jesus also called them to him who would make them into the righteous people of the righteous kingdom. When people heard Jesus call them to him, he motivated them to turn to him to be made righteous so they could enter the kingdom with him as their king. If they had ears to hear, they responded, turned to him, and entered the kingdom of God.

The Word of God is Not the Scriptures

As we think about what the Word of God is, our thoughts may lead us to a common view that the Scriptures are the Word of God. This, however, is not exactly the case. We may refer to the Scriptures as the Word of God because God inspired them. God, however, never used the title "Word of God" to refer to the Scriptures. God used the phrase "Word of God" as a formal title for Jesus. Jesus is the Word of God because he called his people to repent and obey him. If they did, they would enter the kingdom of God. The Word of God as a formal title for Jesus occurs numerous places in the Scriptures. One example is in Revelation 19:13 says, "The name by which he is called is The Word of God." The title Word of God as a reference to the Scriptures, however, never occurs in the Scriptures.

We Give the Word of God

After Jesus died and rose, he ascended to Heaven and sat next to God the Father. However, even though he was in Heaven, he did not stop giving his word. He continued to give the Word of God by the Holy Spirit through his own people. John 14:23-26 says, "If anyone loves me, he will keep my word...the Holy Spirit...will teach you all things and bring to your remembrance all that I have said to you." Jesus continues to give his Word through the Holy Spirit to us as Christians. We in turn speak to other people at certain times according to who Jesus and the Holy Spirit want to hear his Word. Our giving God's Word, however, is not a free-for-all where we say whatever we want, whenever we want, to whomever we want. Our giving God's Word is based on Jesus' discretion for whom he wants to hear his message regarding the kingdom of God. Jesus will continue to give the Word of God through the Holy Spirit to his people all the way until the end of the age. Anyone who believes in Jesus Christ will repent and enter his kingdom.

The Word of God Will Cease

The end of the age will eventually come. It has been coming since the beginning of the world, and it will continue to come. It will move closer and closer each day and each hour. There is nothing we can do to keep the end from getting closer. When it arrives, God will no longer give the Word of God, and no one can enter the kingdom of God. Jesus did say that he was the Way, and no one comes to the Father except through him.

However, a time will come in which a person will not be able to enter the kingdom of God, and the keys of the kingdom which he gave to his people will no longer work.

The Kingdom Will Reign on the Earth

When the end does finally come, all rule and authority changes. The kingdom of God will replace the kingdoms of this sinful world. Revelation 11:15 says, "The kingdom of the world has become the kingdom of our Lord and of his Christ, and he shall reign forever and ever." Jesus the son had been in Heaven at the side of the Father. When the end comes, Jesus will return to Earth and will bring his kingdom with him. No king had ever begun ruling without his kingdom, and Jesus will be no different. He will return to Earth, and we who are in the kingdom will come with him. Jesus, God's son, will then receive the earth as an inheritance, and he will live with us on it for eternity to glorify God.

Jesus Will Receive the Earth as His Inheritance

Most of us are familiar with the concept of an inheritance. We may have received one, gave one, or otherwise knew someone who had. Our understanding of an inheritance may be limited to our place in history and our culture. In other words, we may understand what an inheritance is, but only how it works in our day and age. An inheritance in the time of the Scriptures may be a little different than it is today.

In the time of the Scriptures, a certain man may have owned property. As the owner, he also may have entrusted his property to a manager to oversee it. In doing so, the manager generated revenue or income for the owner. However, if the owner had a son, when the son came of age the owner took the property from the manager, and gave it to his son. The son then oversaw it and generated revenue for his father, the owner. As this pertains to the kingdom of God, God created the world to be sinful and for Satan to rule it. He also created the world so Satan as its ruler would not generate revenue or glory for God. When the end comes, however, God will depose of Satan, destroy him, and give the earth to Jesus his son as an inheritance to rule for his glory. Psalm 2:7-8 says, "The Lord said to me, 'You are my Son; today I have begotten you. Ask of me, and I will make the nations your heritage[44] [inheritance], and the end of the earth your possession."

---

[44] One's heritage is his family culture or history. An inheritance is property or possessions given to an heir after an ancestor's death. In this verse, inheritance is the correct word because Jesus will actually inherit the earth.

Jesus Receives His Inheritance By Way of a Covenant

Prior to God giving Jesus the earth as an inheritance, God foreshadowed it through an earthly covenant that he made with Abram. Many of us who have studied the Scriptures may have heard of the covenants. There were several different types of covenants, and people made thousands of them over the centuries. A covenant was an agreement enacted by one person with another person regarding how their relationship will be conducted. For example, a husband may have made a covenant with his wife regarding how they will conduct the marriage. One man may have made a covenant with another man regarding how they will conduct their friendship. A man may have also made a covenant with those whom he lists in his will regarding how he will bequeath his estate to them after he dies. This latter type of covenant is the type God used to establish how he will conduct his relationship with Abram and his offspring. The covenant God made with Abram was called the Old Covenant.

God's Old Covenant with Abram

God promised Abram that he would make a nation of people from him and give him and his people a particular piece of land to live in. Genesis 12:1-2 says, "Now the Lord said to Abram, 'Go from your country…to the land that I will show you. And I will make of you a great nation.'" God made the Old Covenant with Abram regarding how he will conduct his relationship with this nation called Israel so they could maintain possession of a certain piece of land.

The Old Covenant was conditional, however, as are all covenants. Abram and Israel had to make the true God their God and obey him as the condition of the covenant. Exodus 19:5 says, "If you will indeed obey my voice and keep my covenant, you shall be my treasured possession among all peoples." The "if…then" construction shows that God's covenant with Abram was conditional. Because it was, when God made the covenant, he cut in half several animals and placed each half apart from one another. God and Abram passed between these animals using the imagery of a larger oven and a smaller torch to represent themselves in order to establish the covenant. Though God could not break the covenant, Abram and Israel could. If they did, they would suffer a comparable destiny as the animals. Jeremiah 34:18-20 says, "The men who transgressed my covenant and did not keep the terms of the covenant that they made before me, I will make them like the calf that they cut two and passed between its parts."

To avoid this destiny, God introduced and imposed the law. The law contained rules for how Israel should live as well as for the Temple, the priests, and the religious accouterments. God designed the law to show Israel how to live and how to be cleansed of sin so they could be accepted by God. By obeying the law, Israel could receive and maintain the land God had given them. Joshua 23:5-6 says, "And you shall possess their land, just as the Lord your God promised you. Therefore, be very strong to keep and to do all that is written in the Book of the Law of Moses." There was one major problem with all of this. God designed the Old Covenant so that Israel would break it.

God Designed the Old Covenant to be Broken

When we were children we used things that were meant to be temporary. We played with toy tools and toy dolls that simulated real tools and real children. The toys taught us about the real thing that we would eventually have. Because of this, these things were meant to be temporary. When we grew up, we no longer played with them because we had the real thing. In a similar way, God designed the covenant with Abram to be broken. Deuteronomy 31:16 says, "This people will rise and whore after the foreign gods among them in the land that they are entering, and they will forsake me and break my covenant." God said this as a matter of fact, not as a matter of probability, because he designed his covenant with Abram so Israel would break it. For this reason, many of the aspects associated with this covenant such as the law, the Temple itself, the Temple personnel and accouterments, and the even the land were temporary because God would fulfill them with the real thing. God would give us the real thing through a different covenant. This covenant was called the New Covenant.

God Spoke of a New Covenant

When God had made the Old Covenant with Abram, he made it fully intending to make the new covenant with one of Abram's future offspring. After God made the old covenant with Abram as recorded in Genesis 15, approximately fourteen years elapsed. God then told Abram that he would make another covenant with one of Abram's future offspring. Genesis 17:7 says, "I will establish my covenant between me and you and your offspring after you." The word offspring in this verse is the Hebrew word *zeraka*, which is singular, not plural. This means that it does not refer to the multiplicity of Abram's immediate offspring as some may think. Rather, it refers to one, single, future offspring, a son. Galatians 3:16 says, "Now the promises were made to Abraham and to his offspring. It does not say, 'And to offsprings,' referring to many, but referring to one, 'And to your offspring,' who is Christ." Through this future offspring of Abram, God would make a multitude of peoples come. As such, God changed Abram's name to Abraham, meaning "father of many."

The Sign of Circumcision

At the same time in which God told Abraham about his future offspring, God gave him and his immediate offspring a sign regarding this future offspring. The sign was circumcision. Abraham and any of his offspring were to remove the foreskin of a part of their body from which their future offspring come. As they lived under the Old Covenant, repeatedly utilizing the Temple, priests, and sacrificial system to outwardly cleanse them of sin, they would see in their own flesh that a future offspring would eventually come. God would make a new covenant with this offspring, i.e. Christ, to remove inward sin once and for all. In doing so, those whom Christ would cleanse of sin would become part of the new Israel or the kingdom of God. They would then receive the earth as the reward of the new covenant.

The New Covenant of Jesus Christ

In the course of time, Jesus incarnated himself on Earth, and God established the new covenant with him when he offered himself as a sacrifice to put an end to sin once and for all. Hebrews 9:15 says, "Therefore he is the mediator of a new covenant, so that those who are called may receive the promised eternal inheritance." When God made the new covenant with his son Jesus, he also made it with us who are in his kingdom, just like God had made the Old Covenant with Abram and his offspring. The New Covenant involved God giving to Jesus his son the earth for eternity. Jesus will inherit the earth and share it with us who have become part of his kingdom so that we will dwell on the earth. We will display the qualities of life, knowledge, power, and righteous to a full extent so we can glorify God. Colossians 1:12 says, "The Father, who has qualified you to share in the inheritance of the saints in light."

Seek the Kingdom

Even though we live in this sinful world, we also know that we are part of the kingdom of God. We heard Jesus' Word and responded to it by turning to him. There may be things that tempt us to want to keep living in this sinful world. We may have just gotten married and want to enjoy life with our spouse. We may have worked for forty years and want to enjoy our retirement. However, we are part of a much better kingdom. We are part of the righteous kingdom of God that that will never pass away.

From the very beginning, Jesus sent out his Word into the sinful world about the kingdom of God. We as Christians heard it and have turned to God's son, Jesus as our king. Now, we must wait for Jesus to finish establishing it. Jesus will continue to send out God's Word, and non-Christians will continue to turn to Jesus. They will enter Jesus' eternal kingdom…and there is nothing anyone can do to stop it.

Michael Jones

Chapter 8

How Jesus Came to Establish His Kingdom

At least once a year many of us hear the narrative about Jesus' birth or at least a part of it. Over the years we have heard it so much that it may not strike us as being unusual. However, it was highly unusual in many ways. Jesus had existed from all eternity as a spirit. There was never a point when he did not exist. At the first point in time, Jesus as spirit created everything there is by speaking it into existence. Then, millions of years elapsed. At another point in time, Jesus as spirit created a livable earth including people. Then, thousands of years elapsed. At a still another point in time, Jesus entered this world as a man with flesh and blood like we have. This was unusual because many of us have drawn a fine line between the world we live in and Heaven where God lives. We can easily understand how we move from location to location within the physical world, but Jesus as spirit moving from the spiritual world of Heaven into the physical world of Earth is not quite so easy to understand. However, this is exactly what happened, and it started with Jesus' incarnation.

Jesus' Incarnation

The concept of an incarnation is not hard to understand because it is characteristic to all of us. We have all been incarnated. The word incarnation comes from the Latin words *in* meaning "into" and *carni* meaning "flesh." Each of us has been conceived, and God placed our spirits into our flesh or bodies. However, when we speak of Jesus' incarnation, it is a little different because Jesus was God. God does not normally or even regularly place himself into human flesh. As a matter of fact, he has only done it one time in history. This took place when Jesus incarnated himself.

Jesus originally existed in the beginning with the Father as a divine spirit. In the course of time, Jesus placed his own divine spirit into human flesh. Philippians 2:5-7 says, "Christ Jesus, who, though he was in the form of God…emptied himself, by taking the form of a servant, being born in the likeness of men. And being found in human form." When Jesus placed his own spirit into a body, he incarnated himself. When we think about God, specifically, Jesus incarnating his spirit into a human being, it may raise two very important and distinct questions in our minds. The first one pertains to the more basic of the two, i.e., whether it was even possible for God to become a man.

The Possibility of God Becoming a Man

In approaching the question whether it was possible for God to become a man, it is important for us to keep in mind that God *can* do anything. This may sound like something we learned in Sunday School when we were nine years old, but sometimes we can resolve the most difficult questions with a simple answer. The issue of whether it is possible for God to incarnate himself is simple. He can because he is God, and he can do anything. God the Father through Jesus created all there is. There is nothing which exists that God has not created. Because of this, God can certainly place his own divine spirit into a human body. Mark 10:27 says, "For all things are possible with God."

To understand this, we may find the analogy of a police chief helpful. Police officers within a police precinct assume their posts each day. On a regular basis throughout the year, they will make arrests. They locate a person, read him his rights, and bring him into the police station. However, a rare occasion may arise in which the police chief himself goes out and makes an arrest. When this happens, the news organizations may report on it. When people watch the news and hear about the police chief himself making an arrest, they may wonder if the police chief can do this. They may wonder if the police chief is allowed to go out and make an arrest. The fact is, it is possible because he is the police chief. He runs the police precinct, and he can certainly go out and make an arrest if he wants. With respect to God, he can certainly place his own divine spirit into a human body.

If we want to think about this in a more scientific way, then we can go to science. We may think science opposes God, theology, and questions of faith, but it does not. Though we may never have thought about it in this way, science is knowledge pertaining to God's creation. Because God created everything, true science will simply show the truth about God's creation. Science confirms that every human being is composed of a body with a spirit. Science indicates that we each have a body. Science also indicates that we have some entity within us that causes us to be alive, to reason, to make decisions, and to experience emotions.[45] This entity is a spirit. As this pertains to Jesus, he had and still has a body with a spirit. His spirit, as opposed to ours, was and is divine. The fact that Jesus' spirit was divine, however, does not violate any basic natural laws. There is nothing in science which shows that a divine spirit cannot be housed within a human body. A divine spirit is not any larger or greater than a human spirit because a spirit does not have physical size. A divine spirit is certainly more superior, but this does not preclude God from placing it into human flesh. Jesus can[46] certainly place his own divine spirit into human flesh.

The issue of whether Jesus could be incarnated is related, but distinct from the issue of whether he was incarnated. The realm of possibility and the realm of actuality are indeed related, but they are distinct realms. We can know whether something *can* happen by using our faith in conjunction with reason and logic. Whether something *did* happen, however, involves our faith in conjunction with testimony and evidence. Even though Jesus' incarnation only happened once, we have testimony regarding it. The testimony we have is reliable because it comes from the Scriptures.

The Factuality of God Becoming a Man

When Jesus incarnated himself, he placed all the fullness of deity or divinity into a body. Because of this, we often refer to Jesus as being "fully God and fully man." The Scriptures testify to this in a way similar to witnesses in court. Each witness testifies to something that was said or done. The Scriptures testify to both the words Jesus said as well as the actions Jesus performed. Both indicate that the man Jesus Christ was fully God.

Evidence #1: Jesus' Words

The first piece of evidence which the Scriptures testify to is what Jesus thought of himself. What Jesus thought about himself is very important and the first place to start to acquire information about his divine nature. Whenever we hear a claim about someone, the first person we speak to about it is the person himself. Whether it is a basic claim about who a person is or something he did, we speak to the person himself. For

---

[45] Science is much more than knowledge pertaining to material things. If a person scientifically studied a dog, he would find through scientific observation that the dog is more than a ball of fur with legs. Science would show him that the dog has a spirit that animates him.

[46] The primary tenet of the view called Arianism asserts that God *could not* place his divine spirit into human flesh.

example, if a man claims to a woman that he has climbed Mount Everest, the woman may not know for sure if it is true. To find out, she could review climbing records, air travel, equipment rental, but she would not want to do this first. The first thing she would do is question him about the details. His own testimony would be the first piece of evidence. To discover whether Jesus was both human and divine, we can look to see what Jesus said about himself. In this case, Jesus did indeed claim he was divine. In Luke 22:70, certain Jewish elders asked Jesus if he was the Son of God. Jesus answered the question, "Yes, I am." Jesus' personal testimony strongly indicates the truth. However, a second piece of evidence would make it even stronger.

Evidence #2: Jesus' Actions

The second piece of evidence which the Scriptures testify to is the actions Jesus performed. A person's actions are also a strong piece of evidence in indicating who he is because a person's work indicates his nature. For example, if a man claims that he is an expert mountain climber, a woman could ask what mountains he has climbed. If he has not climbed any mountains, she will know that he is not an expert mountain climber. His claim to be an expert is evidenced by his actions, or lack thereof. When Jesus came to earth, God the Father gave him certain works to accomplish. Only Jesus as a divine being could do these works. These works included healing the blind, deaf, and lame. Works such as these are characteristic of the coming new age, and only a ruler or king of this new age could do them. Jesus accomplishing these works showed that he is both human and divine. John 5:36 says "For the works that the Father has given me to accomplish, the very works that I am doing, bear witness about me that the Father has sent me."

Jesus gave verbal testimony to who he was, and this in conjunction with his accomplishments, is adequate to show that he incarnated his divine spirit into flesh. Most of us as Christians accept the fact that Jesus was fully God and fully man. We live our lives in relation to God believing it. However, if we are honest, we would likely confess that there is one issue we are not completely sure of. Even though the man Jesus was divine, we are not sure if he could sin. We know for sure that Jesus was a real human being just like us. We also know for sure that Jesus did not sin. However, we may not know for sure if he *could* sin.

Jesus Could Not Sin

Jesus could not sin because he had no sin within him. He could not sin in his thoughts, his words, or his actions. We sin in our thoughts, words, and actions because we have sin within us. The sin within us causes us to commit sin. Jesus, however, did not have any sin within him, and he could not sin. It does not matter that Jesus took on human flesh and blood. His taking on flesh and blood would not have caused him to be sinful. Even for us, our having flesh and blood does not cause us to be sinful. The mere presence of flesh and blood is not concomitant with the presence of sin.[47] Jesus, even having flesh and blood, did not have sin within him and could not sin as we do. 1 John 3:5 also says, "In him [Jesus] there is no sin."

This may raise an issue within our minds regarding Jesus' susceptibility to be tempted. Most of us know that Satan tempted Jesus. We also know that Jesus was tempted throughout his life by the same things we are throughout our lives. Hebrews 4:15 says, "One who in every respect has been tempted as we are, yet without sin." This raises the issue of whether any level of temptation could influence Jesus since he did not have sin within him.

When one person tempts another, the potency of his temptation is not contingent on the other person's susceptibility to sin. One person's temptation can still be valid and potent even if the other person cannot fall into the temptation. As this pertains to Jesus, he did not have sin within him, and he could not sin. Satan, however, could still tempt Jesus to sin and obtain something for himself that he should not have. Satan's temptation was still potent and valid toward Jesus even though Jesus could not sin. Jesus still experienced the same temptations as any of us. Satan enticed Jesus to be gluttonous, avaricious, and mendacious, just like he does with us. These enticements were just as potent for Jesus as they are for us because he could receive the same benefits.

Even though Jesus could not sin, he still allowed himself to be tempted. He did this for a very specific purpose that relates to us. Jesus' purpose in allowing Satan to tempt him was to show us that he had no sin. Jesus revealed to everyone the fact that he had no sin by allowing Satan to tempt him and overcoming the temptation. Jesus' receiving the temptation and overcoming it showed his sinless nature. We do the same thing in our daily lives. We may test things that we know are not damaged to show that they are not. For example, if we know our ring is 14 karat gold, we may still test it if we want

---

[47] We will live for eternity on the new earth with flesh and blood, but we will not have sin.

to show another person who is interested in buying it. Likewise, Jesus allowed Satan to tempt him to show us that he had no sin within him and could not sin.

The Kenosis

Before Jesus incarnated himself, he had glory with God the Father in Heaven. When Jesus incarnated his divine spirit, he gave up his position of glory. We see this in John 17:5 which says, "And now, Father, glorify me in your own presence with the glory that I had with you before the world existed." In giving up his position of glory, Jesus did not give up his divine essence[48] nor did he become sinful. He was just as divine as he had been prior to becoming a man. As a man, Jesus still retained his equality with God in essence so that he was still God. When Jesus' gave up his position of glory, we call this the "Kenosis." Kenosis is a transliteration of the Greek word *kenos* which means "empty."

We may be able to understand the nature of the kenosis better using the analogy of a starting lineup in baseball. For most baseball teams, there are a set of starters who are the main players. The starters begin the game and often play for most of the game. However, on occasion a player may get hurt in one game, and he cannot play in several of the following games. In this case, he gives up his starting position for these games, and goes on an injured list. Even though he is on the injured list, he is still a player, and he is still on the team. He does not give these up. In a similar way, when Jesus became a man, he gave up his position of glory with God the Father, but he was still divine in essence. Jesus did not give us his divinity by incarnating himself.

We see a type of kenosis in the Old Testament regarding Moses. The Egyptians thought Moses was Pharaoh's grandson even though he was an Israelite. He lived in Pharaoh's house, and received all the benefits, pleasures, and glory that went along with it. However, when Moses grew up, he chose to leave Pharaoh's house and live with the Israelites. He gave up the glory and pleasures of living in Pharaoh's house to live with his own people. Jesus did the same with God the Father. He gave up the glory that he had with God the Father and assumed the form of a man. In doing this, he emptied himself of the position of glory for us, but he still maintained the same qualities as God the Father.

---

[48] Jesus' essence or substance is both human and divine. The substance or essence of anything is called its *hypostasis*. Hypostasis comes from the Greek words *hupo* meaning "under," and *stasis* meaning "standing." It refers to the foundation or substance of something. Jesus' union of a human and divine nature is sometimes called the hypostatic union.

Jesus Has the Same Qualities as God

God's broad qualities are life, knowledge, power, and righteousness. When Jesus emptied himself of glory and assumed the form of a man, he still maintained all these same qualities. Jesus as a man was still qualitatively perfect and quantitatively infinite, just like God the Father. Colossians 2:9 says, "For in him the whole fullness of deity dwells bodily." When this verse states, "all the fullness" it means that Jesus was still perfect and infinite when he was a man. He was omnificent and could give and take life at his discretion. He was omniscient and knew all things. He was omnipotent and could control the creation. He was immaculate and was completely righteous in all aspects. Jesus the man was fully God and had all the qualities God the Father has.

The Scriptures are full of stories about God's unusual works. Works that go completely against how God normally does things. God took Enoch directly from the earth, and he made the sun stand still. God's sending Jesus who is both divine and human into the world was also unusual. The way it happened, however, was actually very similar to the way we came into the world. However, there were some differences in how he came because he was God. When Jesus incarnated himself, the Holy Spirit conceived[49] his body in the womb of his earthly mother, Mary.

The Conception of Jesus

When Mary conceived Jesus in her womb, it was similar, but not exactly like when our mothers conceived us. We were conceived when our father's reproductive cell united with our mother's. In the case of Jesus, the Holy Spirit supernaturally supplied the seed that Jesus' earthly father Joseph would have normally supplied to fertilize Mary's egg. Mathew 1:18 says, "Now the birth of Jesus Christ took place in this way. When his mother Mary had been betrothed to Joseph, before they came together, she was found to be with child from the Holy Spirit." In doing this, the Holy Spirit created the physical body of Jesus within the womb of Mary supernaturally.

At the moment the Holy Spirit conceived of Jesus' body, the Holy Spirit placed Jesus' spirit within it, and Jesus became incarnated on this earth. Hebrews 2:14 says, "Since therefore the children share in flesh and blood, he himself likewise partook of the same things." Most of us understand that the Holy Spirit supernaturally conceived Jesus in the womb of Mary. Most of us also understand that this was a miracle not unlike

---

[49] The concept of "conceive" means to "originate" or "begin."

all the other miracles God performed. Some of us, however, may not understand how it is connected to Mary's status as a virgin.

The Reason Mary Was a Virgin

Mary's status as a virgin was very important. The historical creeds of the church mention it. Even today doctrinal statements of churches and denominations explicitly state it. It is important to note, however, that Mary's status as a virgin did not *cause* Jesus to be both human and divine. Hypothetically, the Holy Spirit could have conceived of Jesus' body within Mary after she had been intimate with Joseph, and it would not have affected the divine nature of his spirit. His spirit would still have been divine.[50] This may raise the question in our minds of the reason it was necessary for the Holy Spirit to have conceived of Jesus' body when Mary was still a virgin.

Luke 1:31-34 provides excellent insight when it says, "You will conceive in your womb and bear a son, and you shall call his name Jesus...And Mary said to the angel, 'How will this be, since I am a virgin?' And the angel answered her, 'The Holy Spirit will come upon you...therefore the child to be born will be called holy - the Son of God." A correct interpretation of this verse reveals to us that the Holy Spirit conceived of Jesus' body to *show* Mary that her son would be the Son of God. Mary had to be a virgin so she would know that such an extraordinary act of God was indeed true. The idea of the Holy Spirit conceiving of Jesus within Mary would likely have been very difficult for Mary to accept if she were not a virgin. It would raise serious doubts in her mind that the Holy Spirit had conceived the child within her, as opposed to her husband Joseph. Her virgin status, along with the Holy Spirit's testimony regarding Jesus' conception, essentially removed all room for doubt in her or anyone's mind. Jesus was not the Son of God *because* Mary was a virgin. Jesus was the Son of God *because* the Holy Spirit conceived of Jesus' body and placed his spirit within it. The Holy Spirit could have conceived of Jesus in Mary even if she were not a virgin, and Jesus would still have been divine, sinless, and the Son of God. Mary, however, knowing that she was not pregnant by any earthly man, knew Jesus was not a normal man...he was God' son.

Unlike the conception of Jesus' body, Jesus' physical birth occurred like any other birth. Nine months after Jesus was conceived, Mary went into labor. Mary experienced everything that a typical woman experiences during labor and childbirth. Others came

---

[50] Jesus has always been divine and always will be. When he incarnated himself through Mary, her status as a virgin in no way affects this.

Entering the Kingdom

to assist and comfort her. In the course of time, Mary gave birth to the first and only divine man on this earth; the man who as a spirit had previously created her. Though Jesus' birth occurred like any other birth, its circumstances were a bit unusual. We explain the circumstances of Jesus' birth in what is referred to as the Nativity[51] of Jesus. The Scriptures mention numerous details regarding the nativity of Jesus. Two of the more important details are the location and year of Jesus' birth.

The Location of Jesus' Birth

Mary was Jesus' biological mother, but Joseph was not. Joseph was, however, Jesus' legal father. Joseph's family lineage goes back to David and then back to the tribe of Judah who God assigned the town of Bethlehem in Judea. When Caesar Augustus decreed a worldwide census, Joseph and Mary briefly returned to Bethlehem to register their family. While they were there, they stayed in a house, likely with their own extended family. However, the main rooms of the house were occupied so Joseph and Mary had to stay in an area of the house other than the main area. During their stay, Mary gave birth to Jesus. Luke 2:7 says, "And she gave birth to her firstborn son and wrapped him in swaddling cloths and laid him in a manger, because there was no place for them in the inn [living areas of the house].[52]"

The Year of Jesus' Birth

The year of Jesus' birth is uncertain. We will never know with certainly when it occurred until the end of the age. Some may say Jesus was born in A.D. 1, but this would only be based on their assumption that the current method of counting began when Jesus was born. It may not be wise to consider something true based on this sole assumption. We can, however, form a reasonable approximation of the year of Jesus' birth by narrowing down two events mentioned in the Scriptures.

The first event is the death of King Herod. The death of Herod is important because Jesus was born while Herod was still alive, and therefore, before his death. Matthew 2:1 explains, "Jesus was born in Bethlehem of Judea in the days of Herod the king." In addition, Joseph and Mary had absconded to Egypt to wait until his death. After Herod died, they returned to Israel and settled in Nazareth. We know that Herod died in 1

---

[51] The word "nativity" comes from the Latin word *nativitas* meaning the "circumstances surrounding a birth."

[52] The word for "inn" in this passage is *kataluma*. This word has the general meaning of "lodging," and should simply translated "living area."

B.C. because in the year he died a lunar eclipse occurred right before his death, and Passover occurred right after his death. Of the various possible years, in 1 B.C. these two events occurred. A lunar eclipse occurred in January, and Passover occurred in April. Based on this, Herod died between January and April in 1 B.C., and Jesus was born prior to this time.

The second event is the beginning of Jesus' ministry. Jesus was born about 30 years before he began his ministry. Luke 3:23 says, "Jesus, when he began his ministry, was about thirty years of age." To find the date of his birth, we can backtrack from the date he started his ministry. Jesus began his ministry not long after John the Baptist had begun his ministry. John began his ministry in fifteenth year of the reign of Tiberius, which was approximately A.D. 28. Jesus then started his ministry a little after John did. If Jesus was about 30 years of age in A.D. 28, he was born sometime during 2 B.C.

Jesus' Was Not Incarnated Prior to His Birth

When Jesus was born by his mother Mary, it was the first and only time in history that God incarnated himself on Earth. No other time in history did God become a man and perform the ministry Jesus performed. There were, however, instances in the Old Testament when Jesus appeared on Earth in the form of a man, but it was not in his incarnated state. He appeared as a man, but did not exist as a man. One of the more notable instances occurs in Genesis 18:1-2 which says, "The Lord appeared to him [Abraham] by the oaks of Mamre…He [Abraham] lifted up his eyes and looked, and behold, three men were standing in front of him." According to this verse, three men appeared to Abraham, one of which was the Lord. Some Christians may think that because of references such as this that Jesus incarnated himself in the Old Testament prior to his incarnation through Mary. This, however, was not the case.

There are numerous occasions in the Old Testament when God appeared as a man. When he did, he appeared in the form of a man as a theophany.[53] A theophany is not the same thing as an incarnated man. A theophany is a physical occurrence of God where he uses an earthly object in such a way that people know it is God who is communicating to them. In the various theophanies of the Old Testament, the spirit of Jesus simply used the body of a man to appear to one or more people for the purpose communicating to them a message. Jesus used a man's body in the same manner as he used a bush or the wind to appear to someone. When Jesus used a man's body, however,

---

[53] Theophany comes from the Greek words *theo* meaning "god" and *phainein* meaning "showing."

he had not incarnated himself. Jesus incarnated himself into a man for the first time in history when the Holy Spirit conceived of him through Mary.

When Jesus incarnated himself, he had some of the same physical characteristics as his mother Mary. He was related to her just like we are related to our parents and grandparents. Some of us may have seen old photos of our grandparents or great-grandparents when they were young. When we looked at a photo, we may have realized that when we and one of our grandparents were the same age, we looked similar. This is true for all people who are related to each other biologically. It is also true with Jesus. Though we can never know exactly what Jesus looked like, there are things about Jesus' appearance that we can know with certainty because he was biologically related to Mary and her family.

What Jesus Looked Like

Pictures of Jesus abound in our culture. We see them in our churches, homes, and in the media. The problem with many of them, however, is that they are not accurate. They often depict Jesus as either having a European or an African background, when in fact he did not. This may occur for numerous reasons such as a person's ethnocentrism or simply his lack of research regarding Jesus' appearance. Regardless, Jesus' ethnicity was middle Eastern, and specifically Jewish. All of the genetic features which middle Eastern people generally had, Jesus would have had. For instance, his skin would have been darker than many Europeans, but lighter than many Africans. His eyes would have been brown, and his hair would have been dark brown or black. Jesus would have had the types of physical characteristics that middle Eastern people had at the time he was born.

In addition to physical characteristics stemming from Jesus' ethnicity, Jesus would also have physically maintained himself in keeping with godly standards. As we read through the Scriptures, they occasionally address how Christians are to maintain godly appearances. Jesus in his own life would have followed all the commands in Scripture. For instance, Jesus would have eaten a healthy diet, and would not have been overweight or underweight. He would have groomed himself properly. He would not have had long hair because his having long hair would have been a disgrace to him. 1 Corinthians 11:14 says, "Does not even nature itself teach you that if a man wears long hair it is a dishonor for him." Jesus would have also dressed modestly and decently to reflect his inner godliness. He may have worn different types of clothing for different occasions, but he would have always worn them in a godly way. Jesus was the perfect man even when it came to day-to-day issues of living.

Jesus' coming to Earth as a divine man was not a usual occurrence. In fact, it has only happened one time. When Jesus did come, he informed certain individuals of who he would be and the nature of his visit. It was similar to a visit of a high government official. When a high government official visits us and our communities, it is usually a rare occurrence. As such, he usually announces who he is and the purpose of his coming. When Jesus incarnated himself, he sent the angel Gabriel to Mary to inform her that she would give birth to him. Part of Gabriel's message to her was that she would name him Jesus because included within his name was the reason he would come.

The Name Jesus

When Jesus was born on the earth, God gave him the Hebrew name *Yeshua*. Yeshua means "savior" or "the one who saves," as it is a variant of the Hebrew verb *yasha* meaning "to save." God gave him this particular name because he had sent Jesus to be the Savior of the world. When Jesus was on the earth, people called him the Hebrew name Yeshua. However, most of us in today's world call him the name Jesus. This change occurred, not because God changed his name, but because of how our language works.

When Jesus interacted with people, he told them that his name was Yeshua, and they called him Yeshua. The Old Testament never uses the name Yeshua, but the writers of the Greek New Testament used the Greek name *Iesous*. The Greek name Iesous was a transliteration of the Hebrew name Yeshua. Iesous and Yeshua have the same pronunciation and meaning. They only look different because they are in two different languages. Many years later, English translators began translating the Greek New Testament into English. When they came to the Greek name *Iesous*, they transliterated it into English as *Ihesus*. Ihesus is the English spelling of both the Hebrew name *Yeshua* and the Greek name *Iesous*. All three of these words have the same pronunciation and meaning. They look different because they are in three different languages.

Over the centuries, however, the English language changed and evolved. English speakers changed how they wrote some English letters, and they used other letters differently. As such, people began to spell and pronounce the English name Ihesus as Jesus, which is different than the original Hebrew Yeshua. Even though we spell and pronounce Jesus' name differently, we can use it because Jesus himself understands everything that has happened with his name. He understands that his name has been transliterated from Hebrew to Greek and ultimately to English. He understands that over the years, the English language has changed, and we as Christians have not been able to re-compensate for the various changes. He most importantly understands that none of these things have anything to do with malice, deceit, or fraud. It was the natural consequence of language evolution and human nature. Whether we use Yeshua or Jesus depends on the context in which we are speaking and ministering.

Jesus Came into the World in the Way He Did to Bring Us into His Kingdom

One thing we learn when we watch shows about nature is that the various animals on the earth enter into the world differently. Some animals are born into the world. Others enter the world in eggs. There are numerous ways animals enter the world, but God designed each way for the kind of animal he made. Jesus was divine, but he was also a man with flesh and blood like us. He came into this world as God incarnate so he could bring us into the kingdom of God. We could not enter the kingdom unless Jesus came into the world in the way he did. We could not enter the kingdom if Jesus simply appeared to us through burning bushes, angelic visions, or books written by prophets. Jesus specifically came into the world to minister to us. In doing so, we could enter the kingdom of God and glorify him.

Chapter 9

The Ministry of Jesus and What He Did for Us

A local elementary school hosted a kindergarten graduation one year. During the program, the young graduates came across the stage and told the audience what they wanted to be when they grew up. Some of them said they wanted to be doctors, others said firemen, and still others said ninjas. These children may have said what they wanted to be, but none of them really knew what they were going to be. The thing is, however, they were all going to be someone. The parents of these children were doing certain tasks each day for their children that would help them develop into certain people. The parents gave them healthy food, warm clothing, and any necessary medical care. The parents gave them everything they needed to enable them to become whoever they would eventually be.

The same is true for Jesus and us. We were all born naturally sinful. As we lived sinful lives, we did not have any intention to enter the kingdom of God. Someone may have preached to us about the kingdom of God, but we had no desire to enter a kingdom that we did not believe existed. It was, however, God's intention for us to enter the kingdom. Because of this, God sent Jesus into the world to do certain work for us so that we could enter it. Luke 4:43 says, I must preach the good news of the kingdom of God...for I was sent for this purpose." We call the work Jesus did his "earthly ministry."

Background to Jesus' Earthly Ministry

Jesus grew up in Nazareth in the district of Galilee. As Jesus grew up, he attended school, made friends, and eventually began working, not unlike how we all grew up. He performed the work of a carpenter until he was about 30 years old. When Jesus was about 30 in the year A.D. 28, he left Nazareth and went to the Jordan River area to be baptized by John. After his baptism, he began his earthly ministry.

Jesus Proclaimed the Kingdom of God

Jesus began his ministry by his proclaiming that the kingdom of God had arrived, and we could enter it by believing in him as King. Matthew 4:17 says, "Jesus began to preach, saying, 'Repent, for the kingdom of heaven is at hand.'" The concept of repent is based on the Greek word *metanoia*. Metanoia throughout the Scriptures meant "to turn away." When Jesus spoke about repentance in conjunction with the kingdom of God, he called us to turn away from our sin and obey Jesus as King of the kingdom of God. If we believed in Jesus and turned to him as the King, we entered the King's kingdom. If we did not believe in Jesus as the King, we would not turn to him and obey him. As a result, we would not be part of Jesus' kingdom.

As Jesus engaged in his earthly ministry, he had to speak to people who were opposed to who he was and to living righteously in his kingdom. Every word he spoke was God's word, but not everyone accepted or followed it. Because of this, when Jesus gave the word of God and explained the kingdom of God, he used parables.

Jesus Proclaimed the Kingdom in Parables

A parable was a type of analogy. It described a characteristic of an earthly entity to describe the same characteristic about the kingdom of God. A person who heard the parable may have understood the earthly entity which it described, but he had to have faith to understand how it pertained to the kingdom of God. Jesus used parables to hide the message of the kingdom from those whom God would not give faith. Matthew 13:11-13 says, "To you it has been given to know the secrets of the kingdom of heaven, but to them it has not been given…This is why I speak to them in parables."

Jesus hid the message of himself and the kingdom of God in parables so that those who did not believe in him would not thwart his ministry on earth. Jesus spoke openly to those who were his own because they believed in him and would be part of his kingdom. To those who did not believe in him, however, he did not speak openly because they would hinder or impede his ministry. 1 Corinthians 2:7 says, "But we impart a secret and hidden wisdom of God, which God decreed before the ages for our glory. None of the rulers of this age understood this, for if they had, they would not have crucified the Lord of glory." This is like a country giving intelligence about its interests. It openly gives intelligence to its allies who work with it and support it. However, it hides intelligence from its enemies by encrypting it because if its enemies knew it, they would try to thwart the country's actions.

Jesus Revealed the Kingdom through Miracles

As Jesus preached and taught about himself and the kingdom of God, he sometimes coupled one of his messages with a miracle. It is important to keep in mind that Jesus performed miracles for a very specific purpose. Jesus did not perform miracles to increase a person's quality of life, nor did he do so as a supernatural magic show. Jesus had a specific purpose, and it had to do with the kingdom of God.

In some miracles, Jesus controlled nature such as when he turned water in wine, walked on water, and multiplied food. He performed these miracles to show us as a sign that he was the Son of God who created everything and was the King of the kingdom of God. In other miracles, Jesus healed people of certain ailments and diseases, which included casting out demons. He performed these miracles to show us that he could forgive their sin and bring them into the kingdom of God which will be characterized by freedom from sin. In all Jesus' miracles, he showed us that through him we could enter the kingdom and be free from the sin of the current world. Acts 10:38 says regarding Jesus' healing, "He went about doing good and healing all who were oppressed by the devil."

When Jesus preached that we could enter the kingdom of God through him as our King, it initially sounded strange to Jesus' disciples, and they were against it. Mathew 16:21 says, "From that time Jesus began to show his disciples that he must go to Jerusalem and suffer many things…and be killed, and on the third day [within three days] be raised. And Peter…began to rebuke him." However, it was perfectly valid. Jesus the king had to offer himself up to be crucified. This was a must, a necessity, a non-negotiable aspect. For us to enter the kingdom of God, Jesus the king must be crucified.

Jesus' crucifixion would be a punishment. Like all punishments, there had to be a crime that formed the basis to it and that justified it. With Jesus, however, he was not actually guilty of any sin or any crime. So, for Jesus to offer himself up to be crucified, he caused certain events to transpire that would lead to his crucifixion. The first event was that Jesus caused the Jewish religious leaders to be envious of him so they would arrest him and seek to have him crucified.

Jesus' Arrest

As Jesus ministered, he preached and performed miracles regarding himself and the kingdom of God. As he did this over the months, he slowly accrued followers. The Jewish religious leaders noticed this and became envious of him because they wanted the people to follow them, not Jesus. Mark 15:10 says, "He was aware that the chief priests had handed him over because of envy." Their envy became so severe and uncompromising that they wanted to kill Jesus. They did not just want to hurt him, and they did not just want him to stop teaching. They wanted him dead.

There was an issue though. The Jewish people themselves could not kill him. The Roman government ruled over the Jewish nation at the time. The Roman government did not legally allow the Jewish people themselves kill anyone. John 18:31 says, "The Jews told him, 'We are not permitted to put anyone to death.'" If the Jewish people wanted to put Jesus to death, they had to have a capital charge against him. They could then present this charge to the Roman government so they would have justification to kill him. The Jewish leaders attempted to get this capital charge by using Jesus' own words against him. Unlike us, who may be disinclined to speak ingenuously, Jesus was not. He would speak candidly and openly about himself and his activities. The Jewish leaders knew this, so they wanted to get Jesus into custody and question him. They would use Jesus' own words to draft a capital charge against him to present to the Roman government.

The Jewish authorities arrested Jesus in the Garden of Gethsemane just after sunset on a Thursday evening. To the Jewish people, however, it was Friday. After the Jewish authorities arrested Jesus, they brought him into their own custody and took him to the office of the high priest. The Jewish high priest questioned various people to try to find a charge against Jesus. Several charges came forward. The first charge was that Jesus claimed to be able to destroy the Temple and rebuild it in three days. This charge was ultimately dismissed. The second was that Jesus claimed to be a king. The high priest asked him about this claim, and Jesus stated that he was indeed a king. Mark 14:61 says, "Again the high priest asked him, 'Are you the Christ, the Son of the Blessed?' And Jesus said, 'I am.'" Because of this, the Jewish leaders delivered Jesus over to Pilate, the Roman governor, with the capital charge of his claiming to be a king as well as the two supplemental charges of misleading the nation and refusing to pay taxes.

Pilate took Jesus into custody in the same manner as he would have taken any person. Pilate's soldiers held him within an area of the Roman governor's headquarters[54] suitable for an interrogation. The Jewish leaders and the other Jewish people remained outside the headquarters to maintain ritual purity. They believed that if they entered the Roman governor's headquarters, they would become defiled and therefore unable to eat the Passover lamb. Pilate then had to go back and forth

---

[54] Some translations of the Scriptures call this the *praetorium* which is a Greek word meaning "place of the leader."

Entering the Kingdom

speaking between Jesus within the headquarters and the Jewish people outside. Pilate did this in four rounds.

Round 1 – The Initial Charge

Pilate went out the first time to speak to the Jewish leaders and ask them what the charges were. The Jewish leaders charged him with three things; misleading the nation, forbidding the people to pay taxes to Caesar, and claiming to be a king. Luke 23:2 says, "And they began to accuse him saying, 'We found this man misleading our nation and forbidding to give tribute to Caesar, and saying that he himself is Christ, a king.'" Pilate discounted the first two. He went back inside the headquarters and only asked Jesus only about the third charge, i.e., whether he was the king of the Jews. Jesus told Pilate that he indeed was a king. After Pilate contemplated about the nature and seriousness of this charge, he considered Jesus innocent of any capital charge.

Round 2 – The Ramped-Up Charge

Pilate then went back out a second time and told the Jewish people that Jesus was innocent of any capital charge. Because Pilate felt this way, he also tried to get Jesus released. He spoke to the Jewish people about the custom of releasing someone during Passover. They refused and wanted to release a man named Barabbas instead. When Pilate had asked the Jewish people about this custom, it essentially tipped them off to Pilate's intention to release Jesus. So, the Jewish people ramped up their attempts to have Jesus killed. They brought forward one of the previously discounted charges about Jesus misleading the nation, which he had done in his home district of Galilee.

Because Jesus was from Galilee, Pilate sent him to Herod of Galilee who was in Jerusalem at the time. When Jesus arrived in Herod's custody, he questioned him at length, but he could not find any evidence to support a capital charge. Before Herod sent Jesus back to Pilate, Herod's soldiers mocked and beat him. They dressed him up like a king in a royal costume because he had claimed to be a king. They put a royal robe on him, some thorn branches for a crown on his head, and a bamboo stick for a scepter. They bowed before him as an act of mockery. They spit on him and beat him with the bamboo stick. After they were done, they sent him back to Pilate.

Round 3 – The Demand

When Jesus arrived back into Pilate's custody, Pilate went out a third time to the Jewish people and brought Jesus with him wearing the royal costume that Herod's

111

soldiers had dressed him in. Pilate then told the people that Jesus was innocent of any capital charge. Pilate's statement about Jesus being innocent made the Jewish people irate. They demanded that Pilate crucify Jesus. Pilate brought Jesus back in and told him that he could either release him or crucify him. Jesus, however, did not seek or attempt in any way to be released. This is a crucial piece of information. Any one of us would have attempted to be released, especially if we were innocent. We could have just said that we wanted to be released, and we could have walked away and gone on living. Jesus did not say anything like this.

Round 4 – The Placement of Guilt

Pilate went back out a fourth time, and told the Jewish people that Jesus was innocent. Luke 23:22 says, "I have found in him no guilt deserving death." Pilate washed his hands in front of them and told them that if they wanted to crucify Jesus, his blood would be charged to them. The Jewish people accepted this. Matthew 27:25 says, "His blood be on us and on our children!" Pilate then presented Jesus to the Jewish people for crucifixion.[55] Before the soldiers led Jesus away, they took off his "royal costume" and put Jesus' street clothes back on him.[56] They flogged Jesus and led him away to be crucified.

At this point, Jesus' earthly ministry had taken a turn, and he was set to be executed by crucifixion. This change in Jesus' ministry, however, was not a change in God's plan. Everything was proceeding exactly how both God the Father and Jesus desired. Jesus was ready to undergo harsh, painful, and brutal treatment, but this did not mean he did not want it. As Jesus thought about the immediate future knowing what the crucifixion process involved, he desired to continue forward and lay his life down.

Jesus' Crucifixion

In the first stage of any crucifixion process, the person being crucified takes up a wooden cross and carries it to the place where he will be crucified. In Jesus' case, a man

---

[55] The word crucifixion comes from the Latin words *cruc* meaning "cross," and *fix* meaning "to attach."
[56] We may see pictures of Jesus on the cross with the crown of thorns, but this is inaccurate because the soldiers removed the royal costume and put his street clothes back on him before they placed him on the cross.

named Simon carried Jesus' cross. The place where Jesus would be crucified was called *Golgotha*[57] in Hebrew. When Jesus arrived at Golgotha, the Roman soldiers stripped him of his street clothes and cast lots for them. Then they crucified him by attaching his hands and feet to a cross using nails. They put the cross into the ground, so Jesus' feet were about two to four feet off the ground.[58] The soldiers put Jesus on the cross at 9:00 a.m. At about 12:00 p.m., it got dark, and it stayed dark for three hours. At about 3:00 p.m., it got light again, and then Jesus died.

The crucifixion ended, and the king was dead. Jesus, however, did not die like those who were normally crucified. Those who were normally crucified would die because the soldiers would break their legs as they were hanging. Once their legs were broken, they could not hold themselves us to breathe, and eventually they would asphyxiate. However, when the soldiers came to Jesus, they found him already dead, and they never had to break his legs. He had already died because he gave up his own life. John 19:30 says, "Jesus said, 'It is finished,' and he bowed his head and gave up his spirit."

The soldiers pierced his side to ensure he was actually dead. They did this to see if both blood and water came which would indicate he was. The reason for this is simple as a brief look at biology will show. We are composed of both water and blood, with more water than blood. When we are alive, our hearts pump with enough force to circulate blood around our bodies and into all the hundreds of small blood vessels. If we are stabbed while we are alive, blood will primarily come out of our wounds because of the force exerted by our hearts. If, however, we are stabbed when we are dead, both water and blood will come out of our wounds in approximately equal parts because our hearts are not pumping. When the soldiers pierced Jesus' side, both water and blood came out in approximately equal amounts indicating his heart was not pumping, and he was dead.

When Jesus' hands and feet were nailed to the cross, and his side pierced, Jesus' blood was shed.[59] Hebrews 9:13 says, "He entered once for all into the holy places…by means of his own blood." His lifeless body hung limp underneath that glorious title. The spectators who came for the event saw his dead body on the cross. The soldiers stood waiting for the cue to pull the cross back out of the ground and remove the nails. There

---

[57] The Hebrew word *Golgotha* translated into Latin is *Calvaria* and translated into English is "Place of the Skull."

[58] Jesus could not have been much higher, or the soldiers could not have used a sword to pierce his side.

[59] Jesus' blood was shed, not when he was beaten, but when his hands and feet were nailed to the cross, and his side pierced.

was no doubt in anyone's mind that Jesus was dead. Some of us may become emotional when we think about the events of Jesus' death and rightly so. The pain and suffering Jesus underwent; he did it for us. He gave up his own life, denying himself all that goes with life on this earth for us.

When we hear that Jesus gave up his own life, it causes gratitude within our hearts because Jesus died for us. No one else has ever died for us, but Jesus did. In our minds, however, it may raise an issue. It may raise the issue regarding who actually killed Jesus. There seems to be three parties involved in Jesus' death: Jesus himself, the Jewish people, and the Roman government.

Who Killed Jesus?

To discover who killed Jesus, we must first think like a lawyer, and not a caveman. A caveman thinks, "Me hit man, man die." A lawyer, on the other hand, thinks about who is responsible. In the case of Jesus, the person responsible is the one who had the motive and intent to crucify him. The Jewish people were envious of him to the degree that they had motive and intent to kill him. Jesus had ministered to such an effective degree that his rivals developed an intense hatred for him so that they wanted him dead. The Roman government, however, did not have motive and intent to kill him because they deemed him innocent and sought to release him. The Romans did place Jesus on the cross, but they only did this because they ruled over the Jewish people and needed to oversee executions. The Romans, however, did not kill Jesus.

We can see this principle in the analogy of a man standing on a street curb. The man's enemy comes along and pushes him into the path of an oncoming bus so that he dies. There could be two parties responsible for the man's death; the man's enemy who pushed him and the bus driver who hit him. A lawyer will evaluate the situation to discover who is responsible. To do this, he will evaluate the motive and intent of the man's enemy and the bus driver. The lawyer will deem the man's enemy to be responsible because he had motive and intent to kill him even though the bus driver hit the man so that he died.

The Jewish people were motivated by their own envy and hatred of Jesus. Their one intent was to have Jesus killed. For this reason, Acts 2:22-23 says, "Men of Israel...Jesus the Nazarene...you [had] crucified and killed [lit. got rid of] by the hands of godless men." The Jewish people, therefore, were responsible for his death even though they used the Roman government to crucify him.

Entering the Kingdom

This understanding of Jesus' death is not difficult for us to grasp. We see this kind of logic when we watch television shows regarding crime scenes. There is always a series of players involved in a particular person's death. The goal of the authorities is to find who is ultimately responsible. As this pertains to Jesus, the Jewish people were responsible for Jesus' death, and God will charge it against them at the Judgment. There is a twist to this, however. Though the Jewish people were responsible and had Jesus killed, they did not actually cause Jesus death.

Jesus' Actual Cause of Death

When Jesus died, some of us may think his cause of death was exsanguination. We may assume that when the Romans whipped Jesus, it was severe enough that it caused him to eventually bleed out or exsanguinate while on the cross. Matthew 27:26 says, "Having scourged Jesus, delivered him to be crucified." This was not the case. Jesus was not whipped so severely that he bled profusely. When the soldiers whipped Jesus, the whippings did not cause a significant amount of bleeding or possibly even any bleeding which would have ultimately brought about his death. The Romans soldiers intended to impale Jesus alive on the cross, not already dead. Jesus did not eventually die of exsanguination caused by the whippings.

Others of us may think Jesus' cause of death was asphyxiation because Luke 23:46 says, "And having said this he breathed his last." Asphyxiation was the cause of death for the other two men who each hung on his respective cross next to Jesus, but it was not the case with Jesus. When Jesus was impaled alive on the cross along with the two others, the soldiers intended to go and break the legs of all three men. This would hasten their death, as they would not be able to hold themselves up to breathe. The soldiers broke the legs of the first two men, but when they came to Jesus, they saw that he was already dead, and did not break his legs. John 19:32 says, "So the soldiers came and broke the legs of the first, and of the other who had been crucified with him. But when they came to Jesus and saw that he was already dead, they did not break his legs." Jesus did not die of asphyxiation caused by the soldier's breaking his legs because when they came to break his legs, he was already dead.

This leads us to inquire into what Jesus' actual cause of death was. If it was not exsanguination or asphyxiation, it had to have been something. Something caused his death. In the case of Jesus, his cause of death was willful separation of his spirit from his body. While Jesus was on the cross, he determined when he would die and then purposely caused his spirit to separate from his body. This resulted in his death because the body cannot live without the spirit. John 19:30 says, "He bowed his head and gave up his spirit." Jesus gave up his own life, and no one took it from him…and he did it for us! The Jewish people did indeed offer up Jesus as a sacrifice through the Romans. They did so Jesus himself could give up his own life for all of us.

Jesus' Entombment

After Jesus was crucified, Joseph of Arimathea placed Jesus in his own new tomb. Though some Scripture translations indicate that Jesus was buried, he was entombed. Joseph and Nicodemus placed Jesus in an above ground tomb in the rock that could be accessed through a pedestrian entrance. Once Joseph and Nicodemus placed Jesus in the tomb, they covered the entrance with a rock which was held in place by a seal. Jesus had died and was indeed dead. He would not remain dead, however, because the Holy Spirit would resurrect him.

Jesus' Resurrection

After Jesus was crucified on a Friday and entombed, the Holy Spirit resurrected Jesus from the dead on the following Sunday. Death could not hold him in the grave, and it had no power over him. Nothing could keep Jesus dead, and nothing would. God the Father raised Jesus from the dead through the agency of the Holy Spirit. Romans 8:11 says, "If the Spirit of him [Jesus] who raised Jesus from the dead dwells in you." Jesus was just as alive as he was before his crucifixion.

When God raised Jesus from the dead, he placed Jesus' spirit back into his original earthly body. Jesus still had the marks of crucifixion that consisted of nail marks in his hands, a scar in his side, and by implication, nail marks in his feet. John 20:27 says, "Then he said to Thomas, 'Put your finger here, and see my hands; and put out your hand and place it in my side.'" This, however, is not the body Jesus would always have. The body Jesus had between his resurrection and ascension was simply his earthly body having been resurrected and brought back to life.

When Jesus would eventually ascend to Heaven, he would have a glorified body. His glorified body was different than his earthly body. Jesus' earthly body had the genes of his ancestors. Jesus had the genes of Mary, Noah, and Adam. Jesus glorified body, on the other hand, would not have any physical relationship to his earthly ancestors.[60] Jesus' glorified body would also not be subject to the natural decay of the earth or show

---

[60] For this reason, Jesus *was* ethnically Jewish when on the earth, but he is no longer.

signs of scaring, age, and death. 1 Corinthians 15:40, "There are heavenly bodies and earthly bodies, but the glory of the heavenly is of one kind, and the glory of the earthly is of another."

When we think about the fact that Jesus was crucified on a Friday and resurrected on the following Sunday, we may initially assent. Many of us have observed a Good Friday service followed by a Sunday Easter service. Later, however, we may read certain passages and become a little puzzled. Certain passages pertaining to the chronology of Jesus' death and resurrection seem to indicate that the time between Jesus actual death and resurrection was three days. One such passage is Mark 8:31 which says, "The Son of Man must…be killed, and after three days rise again." The Scriptural narrative regarding Jesus' death and resurrection seems straightforward, but Friday evening to Sunday morning is not three days and three nights. We can resolve this apparent discrepancy, however, by taking a closer look at the time-lime of Jesus' death, entombment, and resurrection.

Thursday, Abib 14 - The Day before Passover

The Jewish day began at sunset on one day and ended at sunset on the next day.[61] Each year during Israel's history, the 14th of Abib occurred on different days of the week because it began with the new moon which occurred on different days of the week each year. During the year that Jesus was crucified, the 14th of Abib occurred from sunset on a Wednesday to sunset on the following Thursday. On Abib 14, Judas Iscariot arranged to betray or deliver Jesus to the leaders of the Jewish people so they could kill him. Luke 22:3 says, "Then Satan entered into Judas called Iscariot, who was of the number of the twelve. He went away and conferred with the chief priests and officers how he might betray him to them." As Abib 14 was ending at sunset on Thursday, the Israelites were to slaughter a lamb at twilight or sunset. Exodus 12:3 and 6 says, "On the tenth of this month every man shall take a lamb…you shall keep it until the fourteenth day…Israel shall kill their lambs at twilight."

Friday, Abib 15 - Passover

Passover then began on Thursday evening after sunset which the Jewish people considered the beginning of Friday. At this time, Jesus ate the Passover lamb with his

---

[61] Each Jewish day lasted almost exactly twenty-four hours in length aside from a few seconds because it began and ended at the same time each day. This is similar to modern non-Jewish days which begin and end at the same time each day.

117

disciples. Luke 22:14 says, "I have earnestly desired to eat this Passover with you before I suffer.'" After eating the Passover lamb, Jesus left. The Jewish religious leaders led by Judas arrested him in the Garden of Gethsemane and brought him into their custody. He remained in their custody over-night and into Friday morning, the first day of Passover.

After sunrise on Friday morning, Jesus was interrogated, whipped, and eventually crucified at the third hour of the day, which would have been approximately 9:00 a.m.[62] Mark 15:25 says, "And it was the third hour when they crucified him." Jesus remained alive on the cross until about the ninth hour which would have been approximately 3:00 p.m. At this time, Jesus died. After Jesus died, there was enough time to take his body down, wrap it, and take it to the tomb before the sunset of Friday. Luke 23:54 says, "It was the day of Preparation, and the Sabbath was beginning." On Abib 15, Jesus died prior to sunset and was entombed. This means Jesus ate the Passover lamb and became the Passover lamb on Abib 15, the first day Passover.

Saturday, Abib 16 - The Sabbath

On Friday evening at sunset, Saturday Abib 16 began. It was the Sabbath day, and the Jewish people did not work. At this point in the chronology, Jesus has just been entombed, and the chronology does not pick up until after the Sabbath day is over at sunset on Saturday.

Sunday, Abib 17 – Resurrection Day

On Saturday evening at sunset, Sunday, Abib 17 began, and it was the first day of the week. On the first day of the week, before the sun rose, Jesus rose from the dead. John 20:1 says, "Now on the first day of the week Mary Magdalene came to the tomb, while it was still dark, and saw that the stone had been taken away from the tomb." This verse indicates that Jesus rose from the dead prior to sunrise on Sunday, Abib 17.

This is the chronology of Jesus' crucifixion and resurrection. It does not indicate that Jesus was dead for three days and three nights, and therefore, conflicts with Mark 8:31. There is, however, a simple resolution to this. Mark 8:31 uses the phrase, "After three days rise again." This translation is not as accurate as it could be. It would be better translated, "On the third day." The Greek phrase *meta treis hemeras anastenai* could be translated in both ways, but the latter way is more accurate as it applies to the

---

[62] The counting of hours of the day began at sunrise, though the day started at the previous sunset.

time between Jesus' death and resurrection. Jesus was crucified on a Friday, remained dead on Saturday, and rose on Sunday, the third day.

Post Resurrection Appearances

Throughout our lives, we may have met people who claimed they could heal others. When people make claims like this, we may not automatically accept it until we see them do it. Jesus claimed that he would rise from the dead. People living during the time when Jesus said this may not have automatically accepted what he said until they saw it. For this reason, Jesus appeared to people after his resurrection. Jesus appeared to numerous people to show them that he had indeed been raised from the dead. He appeared to Mary Magdalene, the disciples, as well as to several hundred people. Jesus appeared to these people during a forty-day period until his ascension to Heaven.

Jesus' Ascension

After Jesus' post-resurrection appearances, he left the earth. He completed the earthly ministry that the Father gave him to perform, and he ascended bodily into Heaven. Luke 24:51 says, "He parted from them and was carried up into heaven." The concept of being carried into Heaven does not mean he went into outer space. Rather, God caused him to leave the realm of the creation and enter Heaven, the realm of God. When he arrived in Heaven, he sat down at the right hand of the Father on the same throne of authority as the Father. On this throne, he received the glory he had prior to his birth on the earth.

Jesus Performed His Ministry for a Specific Purpose

We may not fully understand our purpose in this world. We may at times wonder what kind of work we should do, where we should live, and what to do with our leisure time. In Jesus case, he never wondered about things such as these. Jesus came into this sinful world as the King of the kingdom of the God. He had perfect focus on his mission. He performed an earthly ministry for us in preaching and teaching about himself and the kingdom of God. His ministry, however, did not stop there. He also ministered so we could enter the kingdom that he preached about. He ministered by dying and rising from the dead. This was his inevitable destiny, and Jesus was intent on fulfilling it without deviation.

Entering the Kingdom

Chapter 10

What Jesus' Ministry Provided for Us

Some of us have a television service that provides dozens if not hundreds of different programs for us to watch. Some of these programs deal with history and elaborate on the lives of historical individuals who have changed the world in some way. We watch these programs because we like to learn about who these individuals were, i.e. where they were born, how they grew up, and what they did to affect other people. However, when we learn about these individuals, we also learn that the effects each individual has are limited. A certain person may have been the most famous person of his time, and he affected the people of his time to a large degree. However, his effects on us today are very limited. We may still experience them to some degree, but they are limited. Each of these people is like a rock that we throw into a pond. We throw it from one bank, and it creates ripples in the water. Those ripples, though, have very little effect on a person standing on the opposite bank of the pond. All people throughout history are like that rock. The effects of who they were and what they did were limited. This, however, is not the case with Jesus.

When Jesus came to Earth, he was the Son of God who would be the king over the kingdom of God. The kingdom of God would not be sinful like the other nations that had come before it. Jesus himself would rule the kingdom of God with perfect righteousness. Romans 14:17 says, "For the kingdom of God is not a matter of eating and drinking, but of righteousness and peace and joy in the Holy Spirit." We can enter this perfect kingdom because of the ministry Jesus the King performed. For this reason, when Jesus arrived with the kingdom, it was good news. When we read the Scriptures, however, they usually refer to the arrival of Jesus and the kingdom of God, not as good news, but as the "gospel." This is the reason.

The Gospel

We see the word "gospel" in the New Testament gospel accounts[63] of Matthew,

---

[63] The New Testament books of Matthew, Mark, Luke, and John are not gospels; they are gospel accounts. Four different accounts of the one gospel.

Mark, and Luke. Matthew 4:23 says, "And he went throughout Galilee, teaching in their synagogues and proclaiming the gospel of the kingdom." The word gospel in this verse is an English word that began as a Greek word. The original Greek word is *euangelion* which means good news. The Greek prefix *eu* meant "good," and the Greek root and suffix *angelion* meant "message." When English translators read Matthew's original Greek gospel account, they translated *euangelion* into Old English as *goodspell*, or a variation of this. The Old English word "good" meant the same, and the word "spell" meant message. As Old English evolved into Modern English, the "od" and one "l" dropped out. The two words "go" and "spel" merged together and resulted in the Modern English word "gospel," which meant good news. So, when we read passages such as Matthew 4:23 today, it uses the word gospel which means good news. The gospel or good news was the message about the kingdom of God and how people can enter it through Jesus.

Throughout history, many people did not believe Jesus was the king of the kingdom of God. They did, however, believe a righteous kingdom was coming. They had read Scripture such as Isaiah 9:6-7 which says, "For to us a child is born…Of the increase of his government and of peace there will be no end, on the throne of David and over his kingdom, to establish it and to uphold it with justice and with righteousness from this time forth and forevermore." However, they did not believe a man named Jesus, who had lived and died on Earth, was the king of this coming kingdom. Because of this, people began claiming that certain individuals other than Jesus were the king. When they began doing this, different gospels arose.

Different Gospels

In our day and age, we really do not hear much about different gospels. We may hear people refer to the social gospel or the liberation gospel, but these are not gospels at all because they do not pertain to a coming king and his kingdom. They are simply ideologies about how we should live within the sinful world by incorporating Christian principles. A different gospel is a message regarding the arrival of a king and his kingdom other than Jesus. We can see this by reading what the Apostle Paul wrote to the Galatian Christians in Galatians 1.

In Galatians 1, some of the Galatian Christians had turned to a different gospel, and Paul addressed the issue with them. In addressing it, he equated their turning to a different gospel as deserting Christ. Galatians 1:6 says, "I am astonished that you are so quickly deserting him who called you in the grace of Christ and are turning to a different gospel." He goes on to say that there really is not a different gospel, but he had made his point. Turning to a different gospel meant turning to a different person other than Jesus. If the gospel is the good news regarding Jesus and the kingdom of God, then a different gospel is the news regarding someone other than Jesus. This stands to reason since Jesus himself said that there would be false Christs who would come and try to lead people astray. Matthew 24:24 says, "For false Christs and false prophets will arise and perform signs and wonders, so as to lead astray."

People can certainly claim that Jesus is not the awaited king of the coming kingdom of God. There will be people who accept their claim regardless of the evidence we present showing Jesus to be the king of his kingdom. The fact is, however, that Jesus is the king, and when he came, the kingdom of God began. His kingdom will remain for eternity and never be destroyed. Jesus' coming could not be stopped by anyone who ever lived before him. It can never be undone by anyone who will ever live after him. As such, the good news regarding it will never change throughout history.

Though the kingdom of God came with Jesus, none of us were automatically part of it. We were all born naturally sinful and part of the naturally sinful world. In order for us to have entered the kingdom of God, the king needed to transform us from being naturally sinful to being righteous. Jesus did not do this by simply commanding that it happen. It is true that Jesus spoke the creation into being by simply commanding it to. It is also true that Jesus healed a man physically by commanding him to be healed. Jesus, however, did not simply command that we become righteous. Jesus would make us righteous by providing redemption from bondage to our sin, providing cleansing from our sin, and providing forgiveness of our debt to God because of our sin.

Our Redemption

The concept of redemption may be a little hard for us to understand. We do not have anything in our day-to-day lives that we can use as an analogy to reference. We do not talk about anything that has been redeemed except maybe a gift card, but this is not a very clear analogy. So, we have to first look at redemption in the Old Testament.

During much of the period that the Old Testament covered, if one person owed another person an amount of money, the person who owed the money was the debtor, and the person to whom the money was owed was the creditor. The debtor was in bondage to the creditor for the amount of money he owed. If someone paid the money that the debtor owed, the debtor was released from his bondage to the creditor. However, if the debtor was born in bondage to the creditor, the debtor could never be released. The creditor owned the debtor, and the debtor was in bondage for life. Leviticus 25:45 says, "Who have been born in your land, and they may be your property."

This is not a difficult concept to understand. A debtor who was born free, but who goes into bondage can obtain his freedom back by paying the money he owes. A debtor, however, who was born into bondage will always remain in bondage, and the creditor owns him as a slave or bond-servant. The only way, hypothetically, that he could be released is if he died and received a new life. In either case, the person who freed the debtor from bondage incurred a cost in doing so. The person either paid the money owed or gave up something to give the debtor new life. The cost incurred was called a ransom,[64] and it secured redemption for the debtor. The Hebrew word for redemption is *geullah*, and the Greek word is *apolutrosis*, both of which mean "to release from bondage." The person who paid the ransom now owned the debtor, and the debtor became his slave or bond-servant."

God made every one of us to be naturally sinful. We were all born in bondage to sin, and there was no amount of money anyone could ever pay to God for our release from sin. Psalm 49:7-9 says, "Truly no man can ransom another, or give to God the price of his life, for the ransom of their life is costly and can never suffice, that he should live on forever and never see the pit." Because we were born in bondage, the only way for us to be released from bondage to sin was for us to die and for God to give us new life.

God gave us a way to die and receive new life through Jesus. If we die on our own, we are powerless to overcome death and live again. There is nothing we can do. Jesus, however, died and rose on our behalf. When we as naturally sinful people died and rose with Jesus, God released us from bondage to sin. Our naturally sinful spirits died with Christ, and God raised us with a new righteous spirit. Our new righteous spirits were now in bondage to God, and he owned us as his slaves or bond-servants. Romans 6:6-7 says, "We know that our old self was crucified with him in order that the body of sin might be brought to nothing, so that we would no longer be enslaved to sin. For one who has died has been set free from sin." Jesus incurred the cost of his life to free us from sin. Jesus' life then became the ransom payment that released us and bought us. Jesus paid, not for our sin, but for us. He paid with his life to redeem our lives. This is what it means for us to be redeemed. Redemption, however, is only the first part. The second part is purification or cleansing.

Our Cleansing

When we think about being dirty, we often think about our bodies which get dirty as we go about our day. However, many things on the earth are dirty. We just do not realize they are. The water we drink may be dirty if it has impurities in it. The gold rings

---

[64] Ransom means "the cost to release someone."

on our fingers are dirty because they contain impurities which give them their color. Many things are dirty because they have certain impurities within them. Because we were born naturally sinful, we had sin within us. Our sin made us dirty and impure so that we practiced all kinds of sin by nature.

However, when we died with Jesus, God gave us new and righteous spirits. God then cleansed us of sin because all things that God made new and righteous in the likeness of Christ he cleansed of sin. The Hebrew word for cleansing is *tahorah* and the Greek word is *katharismos*. Both of these words refer to something being purified or cleansed. When God cleansed us, he did not undo the sins we committed with our naturally sinful spirits. However, he purified us by causing our naturally sinful spirits to die, and then he gave us new righteous spirits. He removed sin from us so we can begin at that moment to produce the fruit of righteousness, which we were not able to do previously.

In the same way that God redeemed Israel from bondage, and then cleansed her to glorify him, God redeemed us who were naturally sinful, and cleansed us so we can produce the fruit of righteousness for God's glory. Titus 2:14 says, "Who gave himself for us to redeem us from all lawlessness and to purify for himself a people for his own possession who are zealous for good works." This is what it means to be cleansed, purified, or spiritually baptized, but this is only the second part. The third part is forgiveness.

Our Forgiveness

When we sin against another person, one of the more common acts we do to make peace with him is to tell him we are sorry. The person we sinned against usually chalks this up as a request for forgiveness, and he psychologically grants us our request. We and the person we sinned against usually carry on with our lives peacefully. When God, however, spoke of forgiveness in the Scriptures, it was much more than our telling God we are sorry. It was much more than God psychologically granting us forgiveness. It was a matter involving debt.

Because God made each of us to be naturally sinful, we were in debt to God for our sin. God had made us naturally sinful, and we sinned throughout the course of our lives. Each time we sinned God recorded it in our spiritual account based on the seriousness of each sin. At the judgment, we must pay the accumulated cost for our sin as a punishment throughout eternity. Our sins were real. The price we must pay for committing them is real. The punishment will be real. The punishment will be based on God's precise and perfect calculation of every sin we ever committed. He will generate a grand total cost of our sin and convert it into a corresponding punishment.

However, when we died and rose with Jesus, God cancelled our debt of sin. He cancelled it because the sinful people we used to be had died. They were no longer alive. Since God raised us as new righteous people, we are no longer in debt to him. God's cancellation of our debt of sin is called "forgiveness." The Hebrew word for forgive is *salach,* and the Greek word is *aphiemi,* both of which mean "to cancel" or "to pardon." Colossians 2:12-13 says, "Having been buried [entombed] with him…God made alive together with him, having forgiven us all our trespasses, by canceling the record of debt that stood against us." It is important to keep in mind that Jesus did not pay our debt of our sin. He forgave it. There is a big difference between these two concepts.

We can see this in the analogy of a person in debt to an organization. If person owes a large amount of money to an organization, he is in debt and is required to pay it. For him to be out from under that debt, usually one of two things needs to happen. Either he pays off the debt or the organization forgives him of his debt. If the organization forgives him, they simply cancel the debt. The debt was not paid; it was forgiven. As this pertains to God and us, we did not and cannot pay off our debt to sin. Even when Jesus died, he did not pay the penalty of our sin or pay off our debt to sin. Rather, God forgave us of our sin and cancelled our debt because our naturally sinful spirits who owed the debt had died. This is what it means to be forgiven.

When Jesus provided us with redemption, cleansing, and forgiveness through his death and resurrection, he made us new and righteous people. As righteous people, we became favorable toward God and he was atoned. The concept of atonement is one of those religious words we use very seldom and almost never outside of church. However, it is a very important concept when it comes to understanding how our relationship with God changed when Jesus provided redemption, cleansing, and forgiveness.

Jesus Made Atonement for Us

When Jesus died and rose, he made atonement for us and made us favorable toward God so that God accepted us. God's wrath originally stood against us because of our sin, and we were enemies of God, However, because Jesus provided redemption, cleansing, and forgiveness for us, God transformed us into righteous people. God was then atoned or pacified, and he accepted us.

We see the concept of atonement in the Old Testament in the narrative of Saul and Samuel in 1 Samuel 13. Saul was sinful just like anyone else. However, Saul wanted to be favorable to God so he would give him victory as he went to war with the Philistines. For Saul to be favorable, Samuel needed to make atonement for him and offer a burnt offering. Saul, however, offered it himself. When Samuel confronted him about it, Saul said in 1 Samuel 13:12, "I said, 'Now the Philistines will come down against me at

Gilgal, and I have not sought the favor of the Lord.' So I forced myself, and offered the burnt offering." Saul offered the burnt offering himself because he wanted to receive the Lord's favor. Likewise, because of Jesus' ministry, we have received the favor of the Lord, and he is atoned.

The Old and New Testaments each use different words to express the concept of atonement. The Old Testament uses the Hebrew word *kaphar* which means in a basic sense "to cover." If one person sins against another, he may want to hide his sin by covering the other person's face so that the other person does not see or think about the sin. In doing this, the person appeases or pacifies the person he sinned against. For example, Jacob had taken Esau's birthright and then stolen his blessing. After an interval of years, Jacob was about to meet Esau, and being afraid because of what he had done, he sent a gift ahead of him to Esau. Jacob said in Genesis 32:21, "I may cover his face with the present that goes ahead of me." Jacob metaphorically said that he wanted to cover Esau's face with the present because he wanted to be favorable to Esau and be accepted by him.

The New Testament, however, rarely if ever uses the word atonement. Instead, it uses the Greek word *hilasmos* which we translate "propitiation."[65] 1 John 4:10 says, "He loved us and sent his Son to be [make] the propitiation for our sins." Propitiation means to make favorable just as atonement does. When Jesus provided redemption, cleansing, and forgiveness to us, God transformed us into righteous people. In doing this, Jesus made atonement and propitiation for us. We became favorable toward God, and he accepted us. There may not be a formal name to this view of the atonement, but it would be apt for us to call it the *Transformational view* of the atonement because God transforms us from sinful people to righteous people so that he accepts us.

The Purpose of Jesus Atonement and the English Word "for"

Theology and religion can be very confusing to us because of its very nature. It can be even more confusing if we do not understand basic issues pertaining to English grammar. If we do not understand a minor grammatical issue within a passage of Scripture, it can cause havoc within our minds as we try to understand that passage. With regard to Jesus' atonement, there is one grammatical issue that would be prudent for us to understand. The issue has to do with the English word "for."

Certain passages of Scripture elaborate on Jesus' death and resurrection. Some of them use the English word "for" which is based on the Greek word *huper*. The English word "for" can have two distinct nuances. It can mean "on behalf of" and speak about

---

[65] The concept of propitiation is also related to the word propitious which means *to make favorable*.

the purpose of Jesus' death and resurrection. It can also mean "because of" and speak about the reason for Jesus' death and resurrection.

When a passage uses the word "for" as it pertains to *our sin*, it is using the reason nuance. For example, 1 Corinthians 15:3 says, "Christ died for our sins." This verse explains that Christ died because of our sins. However, when the Scriptures use the word "for" as it pertains to *us as Christians*, they are using the purpose nuance. For example, Romans 5:8 says, "While we were still sinners, Christ died for us." This verse explains that Christ died on our behalf as Christians. So as we read in the Scriptures about Jesus' death and resurrection, we can be aware of these two nuances. Jesus died and rose because of our sins, but he died and rose on our behalf so we can die and rise with him.

False Views Regarding the Atonement

For us to really understand Jesus' death and resurrection may not be easy. We are trying to understand how his historical death affects us, and we may not fully understand it. As such, some Christians have developed false views that deviate from the transformational view of the atonement. These views deviate because they teach that we can live righteous lives in our naturally sinful states. These views are prominent because they are not just views we read about in theology books. They are views we hear from the pulpit each Sunday. They are views we live by each day. It is important that we realize, however, that they are false.

False View #1: The Example View

According to the Example view, God sent Jesus to Earth to live obediently and to die as the ultimate act of obedience. No one was more obedient than Jesus himself. God made Jesus' perfect obedience toward him the ultimate example or paragon of how we should also live. When we follow Jesus' example and live obediently as he did, even in our naturally sinful states, God is atoned and will bring us into his righteous kingdom. People who follow this view sometimes use the catch-phrase, "What would Jesus do?" in order to understand how to live.

The Example view is correct in that Jesus lived obediently throughout his life, and we should strive to do the same as Christians. However, the purpose of Jesus' death was not to give us an example of perfect obedience that we should follow in our naturally sinful states. The Example view is subtle because it sounds good, but in reality, it is impotent. People can never know what Jesus would do in any modern situation. People are attracted to this view because they want to enter the kingdom of God in their naturally sinful states without having to die and rise with Jesus. The problem is, they cannot.

False View #2: Moral-Influence View

According to the Moral-Influence view, God showed his love for us by sending Jesus to die. When we see how God gave his only son, it motivates us to love God in return by obeying him, even if we are naturally sinful. When we obey God perfectly, he is atoned and will bring us into his righteous kingdom. Those who promote this view often communicate it by implication. They do not state directly that we should obey God in return for sending Jesus to die, but they may say, "God sent his one and only son to die for us," with an empathetic voice, implying that we should obey God in return for what he did for us.

The Moral Influence view is correct in that God did show his love toward us by sending Jesus to die. Romans 5:8 says, "God shows his love for us in that while we were still sinners, Christ died for us." However, God did not send Jesus to die for us so we would obey God in return. Besides the fact that the Scriptures do not support this view, it smacks of being some kind of divine quid pro quo that God imposes to get us to be obedient in our naturally sinful states.

False View #3: Penal-Substitution View

According to the Penal-Substitution view, God will punish us with his wrath because of our sin. However, God sent Jesus to die and punished him as a substitute in our place. As a result, God's wrath is satisfied, and he will not punish us even though we are naturally sinful. This view initially sounds good. We have our "fire insurance" as some say. We will not receive God's wrath involving eternal punishment in Hell because Jesus paid the penalty for our sin in our place. There is one problem with this view; a big problem. The Scriptures do not teach it.

If we look up various words in the Scriptures such as *paid, debt, penalty,* they never pertain to Jesus' death paying the penalty for our sin. We can look. We can infer that passages teach it. We can even try to make passages teach it. However, our plain interpretation of the Scriptures will reveal that they do not. We as naturally born sinners have indeed incurred debt due to sin which will bring about God's wrath as a penalty. However, God did not pay our debt. Rather, he forgave us of our debt and cancelled it because he transformed us.[66]

Furthermore, when the Scriptures teach the express purpose of Jesus' death and resurrection, they always speak about it as Jesus dying and rising so we can be

---

[66] Jesus paid for us, cleaned us up, and forgave us of our debt for the sins we had done. This is the transformational view. Christians who hold to the penal-substitution view simply merge the first part with the third part. They believe Jesus paid the debt. The truth is, he paid for us and cancelled the debt.

transformed. Colossians 1:22 says, "He has now reconciled in his body of flesh by his death, in order to present you holy and blameless." The purpose of Jesus' death and resurrection is for our transformation, not to pay the penalty of sin in our place. As noble as this sounds, it simply is not what Jesus did. Those who hold to the penal-substitution view may explain that many of the Reformers held this view. This may be true, but the Scriptures do not teach it.

Jesus died and rose to transform us into righteous people and transfer us from this sinful world into the kingdom of God. Colossians 1:13 says, "He has delivered us from the domain of darkness and transferred us to the kingdom of his beloved Son, in whom we have redemption, the forgiveness of sins." It is important to keep in mind that when this happened, we were no longer part of this world. We may be in the world and interact with others in the world, but we are not part of it. The world is heading toward God's judgment each day. The day may be sunny and warm, but it is one more day closer to God's judgment and wrath. When we became part of the kingdom of God, we were no longer part of this sinful world. We are no longer heading toward God's judgment because God has saved us from it.

Jesus' Atonement Provides Us Salvation

God created each of us to be naturally sinful. If he leaves us untransformed, he will punish us on the Day of Judgment. Romans 5:9 says, "Since, therefore, we have now been justified by his blood, much more shall we be saved by him from the wrath of God." There is nothing we could have done to avoid God's punishment. However, because Jesus provided our redemption, cleansing, and forgiveness of sin, he made us righteous. God was atoned and he transferred us from the domain of darkness into the kingdom of God. As citizens of the kingdom of God, we will arrive at the throne of God on the Day of Judgment, and God will save us from his wrath. Our salvation cannot be changed or altered. It is fixed and cannot be undone. As such, God considers us and calls us saved in the present time.

God Saved Us Because of His Mercy and Grace

When we speak about our salvation, sometimes we speak of it in terms of the benefits we get from it. We speak of our salvation as our exemption from punishment, our reception of blessings, and our ability to overcome sin. However, God did not save us just to give us these benefits. He saved us for himself and his own glory. God's saving us was an act of his mercy and favor toward us so we would glorify him. Because of this, Scriptures refer to Jesus' saving us as his "grace." Titus 2:11 says, "For the grace of God has appeared, bringing salvation for all people." The concept of grace comes from the Greek word *charis* which means "favor." God gave us his grace in Jesus because we cannot pay God to get the redemption, cleansing, or forgiveness that Jesus provides us. God gave of his grace in Jesus to save us for himself, and for his glory.

When we speak of Jesus providing redemption, cleansing and forgiveness, our minds may automatically think that he did it for us as Christians. This makes sense because the Scriptures speak about a Christian's redemption, his cleansing, and his forgiveness repeatedly. It is important for us to keep one thing in mind though. Jesus provided redemption, cleansing and forgiveness to everyone. He certainly provided it to us, but he actually provided it to everyone.

The Extent of the Atonement

Jesus provided redemption, cleansing, and forgiveness for every person who has ever lived. Jesus provided these to a person regardless of whether he loved him or hated him. He provided these to a person whether he was a committed Christian or he worshipped false gods. Jesus provided redemption, cleansing, and forgiveness to every person who has ever existed. 1 Timothy 4:10 says, "God, who is the Savior of all people, especially of those who believe."

Though Jesus provided these, non-Christians will never receive them. That is the distinction and the crux of an ages-old controversy. Only we as Christians have received redemption, cleansing, and forgiveness. Only we as Christians have died, and have been made righteous. John 10:15 says, "I lay down my life for the sheep." The sheep here are a reference to us as Christians. However, whether or not anyone receives Jesus' redemption, cleansing, and forgiveness, he still provided it.

We can see the distinction between Jesus' provision and a person's reception through the analogy of a new product for sale. A company may offer a brand-new product to the public. When it does, it is providing it to all people. Some people will evaluate the product and receive it, while others will evaluate it, but not receive it. Regardless of whether some receive it and some do not, the fact remains that the company provided to everyone.

The same is true with reference to Jesus' death and resurrection. Jesus died and rose to provide all people with redemption, cleansing, and forgiveness so they can die to sin and be made righteous. If people do not receive it, it does not affect the fact that Jesus still provided it to them. Some of us use the statement, "Jesus died and rose for all people sufficiently, but only for Christians efficiently," to distinguish between Jesus' provision and a person's reception of his provision.

Jesus Gave Us the Means to Enter His Kingdom

Once there was a fourteen year old boy attended a local church. The boy was a little different than most boys because he worked on a farm, and he was very poor. The boy would come to church in his work clothes, and he smelled like the animals which he took care of. The pastor of the church befriended the boy and talked with him. On one occasion, the pastor received two complimentary tickets to a major league baseball game. The pastor knew this boy had never been to a game like this so he asked him to go. When the pastor and the boy arrived at the stadium, they had to enter through a VIP gate. As they approached the gate, the ticket-taker looked at the boy who was wearing his farm clothes, and he paused for a moment. The pastor immediately spoke up and told him that the boy was with him. The ticket-taker then smiled and allowed both of them in. The boy could not have gotten into the game on his own. The pastor, however, provided a way.

We were all born naturally sinful into this sinful world, and God's wrath stood against us. Jesus, however, provided the means for us to be transformed into righteous people through his death and resurrection. When we are transformed, we can enter the kingdom of God and glorify God forever.

Chapter 11

Jesus Performed His Ministry through Positions

The United States has approximately fifteen different positions in which individuals called secretaries perform services on its behalf. It has a labor secretary, a defense secretary, and an agricultural secretary, among several others. These secretaries perform their services for the nation through their positions which they assume temporarily. By assuming these positions, we see that they have the right and the authority to carry out the functions associated with the position. This principle is similar with Jesus. Jesus performed his ministry of establishing the kingdom of God through various positions which he assumed permanently. By assuming these positions, Jesus showed us that he has the right and the authority to carry out the functions of his position. When we think about the positions of Jesus, we may naturally think prophet, priest, and king.[67] We have heard this somewhat rhythmic phrase so often that we may think of it first when considering the positions Jesus held. Jesus did in fact assume these positions, but he assumed more positions than just these.

Jesus' Positions are Based on Who He Is

All the positions Jesus held are based on who he is. Jesus is God, and we call Jesus God because that is who he is. We also call Jesus the Son of God because he is God the Father's son. God uses the father-son type of relationship so we can understand how he and Jesus are related to one another. God the Father is greater in authority than Jesus and sent Jesus the Son to do certain works and say certain things to us. John 5:19 says, "Truly, truly, I say to you, the Son can do nothing of his own accord, but only what he sees the Father doing." We can be sure that everything Jesus said and did came from the

---

[67] The phrase "prophet, priest, and king" is not in the Scriptures though the concepts are. The actual phrase first occurred in the 1689 London Baptist Confession, chapter eight, number nine.

God the Father. When Jesus began to perform the ministry that God the Father gave him, he incarnated himself and assumed his first position. He became the "Son of Man."

Jesus as the Son of Man

Each of us is a son of man, and it means what we think it means. Each of us was born as a human being from earthly parents on this earth. Ezekiel 2:1 says, "And he said to me, 'Son of man, stand on your feet, and I will speak with you.'" Each of us who has ever lived on the earth is the offspring of a man and woman. They too are the offspring of a man and woman, all the way back to Adam and Eve. When Jesus incarnated his spirit, he was born of a woman and became a son of man. He was born just like any of us were born and became like one of us, a son of man.

Jesus, however, was also "the Son of Man." The article "the" indicates that Jesus was not just a son of man, a human being. He was a special kind of son of man, a special kind of human being. We can understand why he was "the Son of Man" by looking at the background to this phrase.

The phrase "the Son of Man" is a title that comes from the book of Daniel. In Daniel 7, the prophet Daniel had a dream in which he sees a throne upon which God the Father sits. A son of man comes up to the throne, and God the Father gives this man dominion, glory, and a kingdom that will never be destroyed. Daniel 7:1 and 13 says, "Daniel saw a dream and visions in his mind as he lay on his bed...I saw in the night visions...one like a son of man, and he came to the Ancient of Days and was presented before him. And to him was given dominion and glory and a kingdom, that all peoples, nations, and languages should serve him." As God's people studied this passage over the years, they interpreted the dream to be a prophecy in which God the Father will give a man, with flesh and blood like us, dominion over the future kingdom of God. This in fact is what happened.

In the course of time, Jesus became incarnated as a son of man, and fulfilled this prophecy. Knowing he fulfilled this prophecy, Jesus called himself the Son of Man so people would know who he was, and that God the Father had given him dominion over the kingdom of God. Matthew 16:28 records Jesus words, "There are some standing here who will not taste death until they see the Son of Man coming in his kingdom." Jesus incarnated himself into a son of man and told people that he was the Son of Man. God would give Jesus the kingdom of God as its king in fulfillment of the prophecy.

Jesus as Our King

When we think about a typical king, we may have images of a man sitting on a throne wearing a crown. This may be all we can think because we have never lived with any kind of king over us. We have lived with various types of politicians, but none of these functioned as a king. Even what we do know about kings may be perverted, if we live in a democracy and have learned that having a king is tantamount to having a dictator. Fortunately, the Scriptures explain what Jesus as our king is like.

Jesus as our king rules us in perfect righteousness. Everything about how Jesus rules us is righteous. We may be used to earthly rulers who neither understood righteousness nor practiced it when it came to leading their people. However, everything about Jesus as our king is righteous because he is God. Jeremiah 10:10 says, "But the Lord is the true God; he is the living God and everlasting King." Jesus will rule us as our king in perfect righteousness. When we were non-Christians, we did not know what perfect righteousness meant because we were ruled by Satan, the god of this world. He lied to us, deceived us, and certainly did not love us. However, as Christians we can know what prefect righteousness is because Jesus rules us. He will never deceive us, mistreat us, or harm us in any way. Jesus will rule us in perfect righteousness so we can obey him and live for God's glory. We may not realize this, but Jesus will rule us in the most loving way, so God is glorified. The way in which Jesus rules us is like how a shepherd takes care of his sheep.

Jesus Our King is Our Shepherd

In the nation of Israel, kings were often called shepherds because they led and took care of their people who were their metaphorical sheep. 2 Samuel 5:2 says, "The Lord said to you, 'You will shepherd my people Israel and you will be a ruler over Israel.'" Jesus as our king is also our shepherd, and we are his sheep. He loves us and cares for us by giving us the things we need so we can live how God want us to. We may not always get what want we want, but we always get what God wants us to have so we can obey him and live for his glory.

For Jesus to rule us in perfect righteousness, he will have perfect wisdom and knowledge. A king needs to have perfect wisdom and knowledge, so he knows exactly what we need, when we need it, and how much we need. We see this in the narrative in 2 Chronicles 1 about Solomon, one of the kings of Israel. God had made Solomon king in place of his father David. While Solomon slept one night, God appeared to him in a dream and told Solomon to ask him for anything he wanted. Solomon resolved to ask for wisdom and knowledge to rule God's people. Solomon could have asked for almost anything. He could have asked God to give him long life, to kill his enemies, or for riches. Solomon's asking for these things would not have been sinful. However, if he had asked for them, he would have asked for them for his own personal gain. These things would have benefited Solomon, and he would have enjoyed them, but they would not have benefitted the people God gave him to rule. Solomon did not ask for these things. Instead, he asked for wisdom and knowledge to rule and take care of his people. This pleased God very much.

Hearing about Solomon makes us marvel a little because of the rarity of having someone as high as a king ask God for this. Many of us have heard of Lord Acton's famous cliché, "Power tends to corrupt, and absolute power corrupts absolutely." With Solomon, this could not have been more applicable since he was one of the more powerful kings on the earth. However, he still asked for wisdom and knowledge because God caused him to. God caused him to so he would typify Jesus who has absolute power, yet also has perfect wisdom and knowledge to rule us. Jesus as a perfect king and shepherd knows how to rule us perfectly and take care of us. Jesus gives us everything we have, and we lack nothing so we can give God the glory he deserves.

When Jesus incarnated himself on Earth, people knew he was the righteous King of the Kingdom of God. They saw his works and heard his words. They knew the man Jesus, who stood in their midst was the Son of Man from Daniel and the righteous King from Jeremiah. However, they also began referring to Jesus with the title, "Messiah." Many of us have heard the title Messiah, but we may not be sure why we refer to Jesus with this title. We may not even be sure what the title means. The title Messiah does have a specific meaning, and we accurately call Jesus the Messiah. We can see the reason by understanding the title's background.

Jesus Our King Was the Messiah

In the Old Testament, King David set his heart on making the true God his God and obeying him. As a result, God promised David that he would raise up one of his descendants and establish him as the eternal ruler in the kingdom of God. 2 Samuel 7:9-12 says, "I will make for you a great name…When your days are fulfilled…I will raise up your offspring after you, who shall come from your body, and I will establish his kingdom. He shall build a house for my name, and I will establish the throne of his kingdom forever." After David died, Israel waited for one of David's descendants to establish the kingdom forever. While Israel waited, however, they went into captivity for their sin.

While Israel was in captivity, the prophet Daniel gave a prophecy about David's future descendant. This descendant would be a prince or royal son and would bring in righteousness. In his prophecy, Daniel refers to this king as "the anointed one" because when a king assumes rule, he is anointed with oil. Daniel 9:25 says, "To the coming of the anointed one, a prince." When Daniel originally wrote the phrase anointed one in Hebrew, he used the word *maschiah,* which we transliterate as "messiah." For hundreds of years after Daniel wrote this, the Jewish people were waiting for David's descendant. They were waiting for this anointed king or messiah to bring in righteousness. They began referring to him with the proper Hebrew title Messiah or Greek title Christ. When Jesus eventually came, he fulfilled this prophecy and was the Messiah or Christ. John 1:41 says, "We have found the Messiah." This title became the most prominent title for Jesus in the New Testament so much so that the New Testament writers used the name Jesus and the title Christ in apposition to one another.

Jesus the King Established His Kingdom by Dying

Throughout history, if a king went to war with another country and conquered it, he became king over it. The people of the conquered king became his people. This was very similar to how Jesus established his kingdom. Jesus established the people of his kingdom by taking the people of this sinful world and making them his people. Any of us who have been saved were at one time part of the sinful world. Jesus took us from the sinful world and placed us into his kingdom. However, here is where the irony comes in. Jesus established us in his kingdom by dying for us. This may seem like the opposite of what a king does to establish his kingdom, but with Jesus it is not. Jesus saved us and placed us into his kingdom by dying for it. Zechariah 13:7 says, "Strike the Shepherd, and the sheep will be scattered…I will say, 'They are my people'; and they will say, 'The Lord is my God.'" For this reason, as Jesus stood in the presence of Pilate, he proclaimed his identity as the highest king, even though he knew he would die in the next few hours. This leads us to Jesus' position as Savior.

Jesus as Our Savior

When we think of a king being a savior, our thoughts may turn to stories of a king marching with his army toward his enemy. He engages his enemy in battle and ultimately wins through a strenuous and lengthy battle. This is not how Jesus saved us though. Jesus our king became our savior by dying and rising for us. No historical earthly king has ever done this for his people, but Jesus did. Jesus died and rose as our king to make us righteous. Because Jesus made us righteous, God transferred us from the sinful world into the Kingdom of God. Having gone through this transfer, God saved us from his wrath which he will dispense on the Day of Judgment. Jesus then has become our Savior. We can see the way in which Jesus is our savior through the Old Covenant symbolism of the high priest and the sacrifice he offered for sin.

Jesus as Our High Priest

We often think of Jesus as being a priest, and this is correct. More specifically, however, he was a high priest. For us to understand the work Jesus accomplished for us as our high priest, we can look to the earthly high priests who functioned under the old covenant. The Old Covenant high priests functioned to foreshadow Jesus as the true high priest. Earthly high priests functioned in an earthly temple. God's people went to the temple to worship him, praise him, pray to him, and offer gifts to him. Prior to their doing this, the high priest offered sacrifices because of his own sins as well as for the sins of the people. Hebrews 5:1 says, "For every high priest chosen from among men is appointed...to offer gifts and sacrifices for sins." When the high priest offered gifts and sacrifices because of sin, his work and the sacrifices themselves pointed us to Jesus Christ as our true high priest.

Jesus as the one true high priest offered himself as a sacrifice that took away our sin once for all. Hebrews 9:12 says, "He entered once for all into the holy places, not by means of the blood of goats and calves but by means of his own blood., thus securing eternal redemption." Jesus was both the high priest and the sacrifice whose blood he carried. Through Jesus' work as our high priest, he provides us with redemption, cleansing, and forgiveness of sin. We can be transformed from naturally sinful people to righteous people. We can be saved from punishment and can enter the kingdom of God. Hebrews 5:9 says, "He became the source of eternal salvation." As people of the kingdom of God, we can begin to worship God, praise him, pray to him, and offer gifts to him with a sincere heart and right motives.

Jesus as Both Our High Priest and King

Throughout history, a king did not normally get involved in the religious affairs of his nation. It is true that in some time periods, the church and the state were closely aligned. However, even in these instances kings did not usually function in religious positions. This changed with Jesus. Under the old covenant, earthly men assumed the position of king, and different earthly men assumed the position of high priest. With Jesus they merged together. There is a prophecy in the Old Testament regarding these two positions merging in Jesus.

The prophecy is given by Zechariah. When Zechariah gave the prophecy, Jerusalem and Israel had almost been completely destroyed because of their sins. God, however, would not destroy them completely. So, God took a high priest named Joshua and used him to rebuild Jerusalem in the way that a king would. Because he used a high priest to rebuild the city of God, he says of him in Zechariah 6:12-13, "The man whose name is the Branch: for he shall branch out from his place...It is he who shall build the temple of the Lord and shall bear royal honor, and shall sit and rule on his throne. And there shall be a priest on his throne, and the counsel of peace shall be between them both." The prophecy pertained to a priest who would rule as king over Israel. When Jesus came, he fulfilled this prophecy. Jesus became both our king and high priest, and through his ministry, he rebuilt the New Jerusalem, which is us.

It is not uncommon for a person of some importance to use another person to speak on his behalf. The president uses a press secretary, and a CEO uses a public relations representative. These types of individuals directly receive information from their superiors and give it to others on their behalf. As God has worked in the world to establish his kingdom, he has done the same thing. He has used certain people to speak on his behalf regarding what he is doing. These individuals were called prophets. When Jesus came to perform his ministry regarding himself and the kingdom of God, he also functioned as a prophet.

Jesus as Prophet

A prophet is a person whom God appointed to speak on his behalf. The word prophet is based on the Hebrew word *nabi* meaning "spokesman" and the Greek word *prophetes* meaning "speak before." God would give a prophet a message, and the prophet would go before others to speak the message as God's spokesman. Jeremiah 1:5-7 says, "I have appointed you a prophet to the nations...and all that I command you, you shall speak." For the prophets to confirm their message, God sometimes gave the prophets the power and ability to perform a miracle. A miracle was a supernatural demonstration of God's power related to his message about what he will do. A prophet would give God's message to his intended recipients and perform a miracle confirming to them that the message was true.

Jesus was a prophet, and he spoke the words the Father gave him to speak to those whom the Father wanted to receive his message. John 17:8 says, "The words which you gave me, I have given to them." Jesus gave numerous types of messages to people as God's word. Some were commands to obey him, and some were promises of either blessing or judgment based on how the people responded. When Jesus gave a particular message, he sometimes healed people to indicate the veracity of his message.

God the Father indicated that Jesus was a prophet in several passages. A notable one is when God the Father called Jesus to a mountain. On the mountain, Jesus spoke with Moses and Elijah, two other prophets. At one point, God the Father spoke to Moses and Elijah regarding Jesus. He said according to Matthew 17:5, "This is my beloved son, with whom I am well-pleased; listen to him." In saying this, he signified that Jesus is a prophet like Moses and Elijah, and they should listen to him. The facts that prophets were sent by God and spoke his words reveal that they were very similar to another position, namely that of an apostle.

Jesus as Apostle

When we speak of an apostle, however, it is a little different than a prophet. In a general sense, an apostle was a man whom someone sent to do something or to complete an objective. The position of apostle sometimes had requirements necessary for one to assume the position. The word apostle comes from the Greek words *apo* meaning "from" and *stello* meaning "to depart." The most common analogy would be government agents whom the government sends to complete various objectives such as gather intelligence or deliver items of value. Historically, there were many different types of apostles whom people sent to complete various objectives.

God himself also had apostles. God's apostles were men God sent to build the kingdom of God through the preaching of the gospel. For them to do this, God required that the apostles had witnessed Jesus' resurrection. Acts 1:22 says regarding the requirements of an apostle, "One of these men must become with us a witness to his resurrection." When we think about apostles, we usually think about the twelve that were present on the Day of Pentecost. After we research the Scriptures, we see that there were several others such as Paul and Timothy. There was one apostle, however, that came before any of these. It was Jesus himself. Jesus was the first apostle whom God the Father sent to present himself alive to others and preach the gospel of the kingdom of God. Hebrews 3:1 says, "Consider Jesus, the Apostle and High Priest of our confession."

Jesus Had Different Descriptors

When we speak about another person, we do not usually refer to him using descriptors. We will call the person by name or even by position, and that is about it. However, when God spoke of Jesus, he used many different descriptors in both the Old and New Testaments. The reason for this is simple. Names are simply a mixture of letters to form a sound that we connect with a person. When we say the name John or Mary, others connect these sounds to certain people. Descriptors, however, function much differently. Descriptors indicate someone's identity or his work. God spoke of Jesus using different descriptors to describe the importance of Jesus identity and his work. God referred to Jesus in the Old Testament with certain descriptors such as "Immanuel" in Isaiah 7:14. God also referred to Jesus in the New Testament with certain descriptors such as "The bread of life" in John 6:35. God used numerous descriptors such as these to describe the importance of Jesus identity and work. Jesus was not simply a person with a name. He was so much more and did so much more. It is important to keep in mind that the various descriptors were not positions Jesus assumed. Jesus assumed certain positions permanently because he had the right and authority to carry out the various functions of his positions. The functions Jesus performed in these positions allowed us to enter the kingdom of God.

Many of us use a computer to do our jobs within the organization we work for. Occasionally, we may have a problem with our computer and will need the assistance of the staff member who maintains the organization's computers. We usually do not call him "the guy who maintains the computers," however. He has an official title. His title is something like the "Information Technology Specialist." Many organizations have employees with titles like these. To people outside the organization, the titles may sound fancy. To those of us within, they are not. We all have titles like this so people know who we are and what we are authorized to do. The same thing is true with Jesus. Jesus as God's Son came to Earth to be the king over the kingdom of God. He assumed different positions to do this, and because he did, we know who he was and what he did to make us righteous so we could enter the kingdom.

Chapter 12

What God Did to Bring Us to Jesus and into His Kingdom

There are many different genres of movies. There is drama, comedy, and romance, among several others. Screenwriters write movies within one genre differently than they do movies within other genres. For example, in a romance movie, they want to show how a man and a woman came together. They elaborate on the various circumstances that drew the man and woman to each other, then drove them apart, and finally brought them back together again. Some of us like to watch romance movies because they show the circumstances in which two people fell in love and got married.

When each of us became righteous and entered the kingdom of God, it involved a narrative not unlike a romance movie. Jesus provided us with redemption, cleansing, and forgiveness so we could become righteous and enter the kingdom of God. However, when Jesus provided these three things, we did not automatically receive them. Our receiving them involved God working in our lives to bring us to Jesus. God worked to cause certain things to happen to us so that we would eventually receive Jesus' provision of redemption, cleansing, and forgiveness. The first thing God did was to choose us.

God Chose to Make Us Righteous

There are many things God did to bring us to Jesus, but prior to doing any of them, God chose us. God had to choose us because in order for him to begin working in our lives, he must have chosen the object of his work. Ephesians 1:4 says, "He chose us in him before the foundation of the world." When we think about the fact that God chose us before he made the world, we may realize that God chose us before he even made us. Before God made the world and even before he made us, he decided that he would eventually create each of us to exist at a certain time in history. He also decided that after he created us, he would transform us from being sinful to being righteous at a certain point in our lives. God chose to do both of these acts together prior to his creating the world and even before he created us.

When we think about issues such as these, timing is everything, literally. We live in a world that is chronological, and we think about when things occurred chronologically. As we think about God's choosing us, we can be sure that God did not choose to create us, but then after sin entered the world, chose to make us righteous.[68] Rather, long before God created us, he chose to eventually create us sinful as well as to eventually recreate us righteous. This is similar to a youth baseball team. Before the players even met for practice or games, the team manager chose them. The players themselves or their parents had no say on whether they got chosen. Aside from bribing the team manager or otherwise coercing him, the players could not have done anything to get chosen. The choice for them to be on the team was solely up to the manager, and it happened before they even attended their first practice or played their first game. In a similar way, before we even existed, God chose to eventually create us with the intent to eventually make us righteous. For this reason, the Scriptures refer to us with four designations. They call us chosen, predestined, elected or appointed. Acts 13:48 says, "As many as were appointed to eternal life believed." All four of these terms mean the same thing.

God Chose to Keep Others Unrighteous

In the same way God chose to make us righteous, he also chose to keep others unrighteous. Before God created the world, he chose the eternal and specific destiny of all people. He chose to make us righteous as our destiny. He also chose to keep others unrighteous as their destiny. Proverbs 16:4 says, "The Lord has made everything for its purpose, even the wicked for the day of trouble." There is nothing the unrighteous can do to become righteous because God chose them to remain unrighteous, and he keeps them unrighteous. Some people call this "double predestination," but the word double is unnecessary because all things have been destined for some end.[69]

---

[68] In theological circles, we explain this basic concept with two technical terms. One is called infralapsarianism, which means *after* or *under* [infra] *the fall* [lapse]. In infralapsarianism, God chose to make people righteous after Adam sinned because he could not anticipate that Adam would sin. The other is called supralapsarianism, which means *before* or *above* [supra] *the fall* [lapse]. In supralapsarianism, God chose to make certain people righteous before Adam sinned, and even before the creation because he knew Adam would sin. Supralapsarianism is correct.

[69] The phrases "predestination of the righteous" and "predestination of the unrighteous" are more accurate.

When some of us hear about God's choosing to make us righteous and choosing to keep others unrighteous, we may wonder whether God is unjust in doing this. What makes someone just is whether he is right in doing something. So, the issue is more aptly whether God is right to choose to make us righteous and keep others unrighteous. One response would be to say that it is right because God chooses to do this, and anything God chooses to do is right. This answer would be correct and adequately supported in Scripture. Romans 9:11 says, "For though they were not yet born and had done nothing good or bad – in order that God's purpose of election might continue, not because of works but because of him who calls." However, when we hear this response and even read the supporting verses, we may agree, but we still want more of an explanation. We want to know why this is right for God to do.

Why God Predestined People Differently

When we deal with the issue of why God makes some people righteous and keeps others unrighteous, it is important to think about his purpose or end in doing it. Everything God does is right, but everything God does is also done to bring glory to himself. God chooses to make us righteous, but chooses to keep others unrighteous to bring glory to himself. God receives glory by comparing those whom he has made righteous with those whom he has kept unrighteous. God has destined the unrighteous to receive his wrath so he keeps them unrighteous. He also allows them to remain in the world so that they can be compared to the righteous. Romans 9:22-23 says, "What if God, desiring to show his wrath and to make known his power, has endured with much patience vessels of wrath prepared for destruction, in order to make known the riches of his glory for vessels of mercy, which he has prepared beforehand for glory." When we whom God made righteous live around those whom he has kept unrighteous, there is a noticeable distinction. Our righteous character is compared to the character of the unrighteous in various situations and contexts. The difference serves as a means to glorify God. God's power and majesty is revealed through his work toward us, and he is glorified.

This was the reason Moses did not want the Israelites destroyed for their sin. God had brought the Israelites out of Egypt, but they sinned, and God could have destroyed them. If God did, he would not be glorified for bringing them out. The people of the world may have thought he was powerless. Numbers 14:15-16 says, "Now if you kill this people as one man, then the nations who have heard your fame will say, 'It is because the Lord was not able to bring this people into the land.'" As a result Moses interceded for the Israelites, and asked God to pardon them. God did. However, God did not pardon them for their benefit, but for his glory. Numbers 14:20-21 goes on to say, "Then the Lord said, 'I have pardoned, according to your word. But truly, as I live, and as all the earth shall be filled with the glory of the Lord.'" God pardoned the Israelites so that as he worked in them within the world and fulfilled his promises to them, he compared them to others. The way God worked with Israel would reflect back on him for his glory. In the same way, God also makes us righteous and keeps others unrighteous so when people see the two groups and compare them, God is glorified.

This may be easier to understand through the analogy of a football team. There are many things in the world that have glory, but they are only seen to have glory because they are contrasted with things that do not. Without the contrast, people would not see their glory. For example, a football team competes against another football team. When it plays better and wins, it has glory. We can see its glory because it is contrasted with the other team through the competition. Without the competition, we could not see the glory. The same thing is true with God. God makes us righteous, and keeps other people unrighteous and living in the world. As people see our excellence and honor as righteous people in contrast to the baseness and dishonor of unrighteous people, they see God's glory through his work toward us.

When we think about the moment when God chose us, it is a little mind-boggling. It occurred outside of the current dimension. We cannot say when God chose us or where he did. All we know is that he did long before he every made anything. No one could have done anything anywhere, including us, to affect God's choice to eventually place us on the earth and make us righteous. However, in eventually making us righteous, God did not do it automatically. God did not cause us to be born righteous or even become righteous on our own. God made us righteous by bringing us to Jesus. God's first step in bringing us to Jesus included our hearing about him.

God Ensured We Heard about Jesus

In order for any of us to have initially believed in Jesus, we must have first heard about him. We would have only believed in Jesus by hearing about who he is and what he has done. Romans 10:14 says, "And how are they to believe in him of whom they have never heard?" When God chose to create us with the intention of making us righteous, he planned our lives in such a way that we would hear about Jesus at some point. Because of this, God caused another Christian to tell us the gospel. Acts 1:8 says, "You will be my witnesses in Jerusalem and in all Judea and Samaria, and to the end of the earth.'" In this passage, God used the apostles who had witnessed Jesus' resurrection. For us, God used another Christian to speak or even write about Jesus. He may have used a Christian to speak at an evangelistic crusade or he may have planned that a Christian write a book that we would read so that we learned about Jesus. God may have even caused us to remember the gospel which a Christian had previously preached to us, as opposed to directly hearing it. Regardless of how we heard about Jesus, God planned that we would.

When God chose us in the distant past, his decision was fixed. As the millions of years elapsed prior to God making the earth livable, he did not change his mind. As the hundreds of years elapsed after he made the earth livable, he still did change his decision. Even after we were born and began sinning each day against him, he did not get mad and alter his decision about us. Even if we were to ask God in a prayer to reject us and tell him that he was not our God, even then he would not withdraw his decision to make us righteous. We have such a wonderful God who is worthy to be praised! This does, however, raise an issue. The issue has to do with why we even needed to hear the gospel about Jesus and the kingdom of God.

Why We Needed To Hear the Gospel since God Predestined Us

We needed to have heard the gospel because hearing it was part of God's plan to make us righteous. God chose us long before he created us, and this was part of his plan. God also caused us to hear the gospel of Jesus at some point in our lives, but this also was part of his plan. Both aspects were part of God's plan.

When we think about how God works, it is important to realize that God has a plan that he is working out in both our lives and in the world. Everything that God does such as initially choosing us, saving us on the Day of Judgment, and every single thing in between is part of his plan.

To understand this, the analogy of a college admissions representative may be helpful. God undoubtedly calls each person to do certain types of work. As such, he may lead each of them to a particular college to acquire training and credentialing. However, God may also use an admissions representative of that school in order to tell that person about the college. Even though God will undoubtedly lead the person to that college, he still *used* the admissions representative from that college in the process of bringing that person to the college. God's bringing the person to the college and God's using the admissions representative were both part of his plan. In a similar way, God chose to eventually make us righteous through Christ. This was part of his plan for us. However, his using a Christian to tell us about the gospel so we could believe was also part of his plan.

When God caused others to preach to us the gospel of Jesus and the kingdom, we sometimes refer to this as his "burdening" them. The metaphorical concept of God's burdening a Christian means God called him to fulfill certain responsibilities which often includes preaching the gospel. We use the concept of "burdening" because it is a responsibility or obligation that God has placed on him like a burden. If he does not fulfill the responsibility, he will have a sense of guilt. We see this with the Apostle Paul who stated in 1 Corinthians 9:16, "For necessity is laid upon me. Woe to me if I do not preach the gospel!" The concept of a woe pertains to pain or displeasure. Paul stated this because God had called him to preach the gospel, and if he did not obey, God would have brought discipline on him. God called Paul as well as many of us as Christians to preach the gospel because he was working in the lives of those whom he had chosen long before he made the earth.

Many of us have heard of God's plan. Often we hear about it from preachers and teachers who desire to encourage us. They tell us that God has a plan for our lives. This is completely true. God not only has a plan, but he also works in our lives to achieve it. When we hear about God's plan, we may presume it ends when it comes to God's choosing us. In other words, God chooses us, and then everything after that is up to us. This not the case, and just the opposite is true. God's choosing us is just the beginning.

God Gave Faith to Those Whom He Had Chosen

Because God had chosen us, at some point in our lives he gave us faith. 2 Peter 1:1 says, "To those who have received a faith of the same kind as ours." The moment when God gave us our initial faith was not arbitrary. There was a specific kind of time when God gave us faith for the very first time. God gave it to us during a hearing of the gospel. We may have heard the gospel many times during our lives, or we may have only heard it one time. Regardless, the point when God initially gave us faith to believe in Christ was during one of these gospel hearings (or afterwards when we remembered it). Romans 10:17 says, "So faith comes from hearing, and hearing through the word of Christ." God did not give any of us faith to believe in Christ without our hearing the gospel.[70] We may have heard about God's love, his power, and his holiness, among

---

[70] Sermons have been preached that have omitted the gospel, and not a single person received faith when they heard them.

other things. However, we never received initial faith when we heard these topics because God only gave us initial faith in Jesus when we heard about him. For this reason, the last thing each of us ever did as a non-Christian was to think about the gospel of Jesus Christ.

The faith God gave us was a real entity. God actually gave us something that we did not have before. The English word "faith" comes from the Hebrew word *emunah* and the Greek word *pistis*. These two words mean "belief about something that is not based on earthly evidence." Hebrews 11:1 says, "Now faith is the assurance of things hoped for, the conviction of things not seen." When God initially gave us faith in Jesus, our faith convinced us to believe in Jesus so we would follow him in his death and resurrection, and he would make us righteous. Romans 3:21-22 says, "But now the righteousness of God has been manifested...the righteousness of God through faith in Jesus Christ for all who believe." Once God made us initially righteous, he continued making us more righteous by causing our faith to grow. God caused our faith to grow when we exercised the faith he had already given us. James 2:22 says, "You see that faith was active along with his works, and faith was completed by his works." As God caused our faith to grow, we began living more righteously than we had been living. This what we refer to as "spiritual growth."[71]

When we hear that God gave us faith, this may seem strange to us at first. We may have been accustomed to hearing that we should generate our own faith. We have heard preachers and teachers tell us to "just have faith" or "just believe." The fact is, however, that we did not and cannot generate faith on our own. Any level or degree of faith must come from God himself.

We Could Not Have Generated Our Own Faith

We cannot generate our own faith in Jesus because our faith is a belief that comes, not from earthly evidence, but from God himself. Earthly evidence proves things pertaining to the earth such as the facts that gravity will pull us to the ground and two plus two equals four. Faith, however, proves things pertaining to things unseen, and that pertain to God. We believe that Jesus was the Messiah because of the faith God gave us. We believe that God created us from Adam and Eve as opposed to single cell organisms because of the faith God gave us. We believe many things that earthly

---

[71] This means spiritual growth comes about when God causes a person's faith to grow because he used the level of faith God had already given him. Christianity is not a static religion. It is a dynamic religion that requires us to continually use the faith God had given us.

evidence cannot prove to us because of the faith God gave us. God must give it to us in order for us to believe it. As such, we cannot self-generate faith on our own regarding who Jesus is and his kingdom.

We may have the notion that we can generate our own faith because of how some Bible versions translate certain passages of Scripture. One notable passage is Mark 11:22. Some Bible versions translate this verse as, "And Jesus answered them, 'Have faith in God.'" On its face, this passage incorporates the imperative tense and is telling us to have faith. We then interpret the verse as teaching that we should generate our own faith. This, however, is not how the passage should have been translated. The passage should have been translated using the present tense to say, "You have faith in God." We could then interpret it to mean that we have faith because God gave it to us based on what he will do. If we translate and interpret the verse this way, it makes the verses that follow after it make much more sense.

In the following verses, we have a metaphor regarding a mountain. We can only understand the metaphor if we first understand the actual meaning of the previous verses. The actual meaning of Mark 11:22 is that God has given us faith, and we have faith. If God chooses to do something through us, even if it means moving a mountain, he will give us faith that he will do it. Because of our faith, we will then work with him and move the mountain. God decides what to do first, and then gives us faith so we understand what he will do and work with him. If, however, we interpret Mark 11:22 as "have faith," meaning it is telling us to self-generate our faith, then we can actually do anything we want. We can just force ourselves to believe that we can move a mountain, and God will comply with our self-generated faith by moving it. This, however, is not only an incorrect interpretation of the verse, but it is not how God works. We cannot generate our own faith, and then expect God to do what we had forced ourselves to believe. If this were actually the case, the geological landscape of the earth would be quite different.

As we think about our faith, we may sometimes wonder how it affects us. We read about all those individuals in Hebrews 11 and 12 whose faith made them righteous and caused them to do amazing things as a testimony to God. We may sometimes think about how our faith causes us to become righteous and enable us to obey God in ways we never thought we could. The answer to this is that our faith does not make us righteous. God does. God makes us righteous because of Jesus through faith that he gave us which caused us to follow him.

Our Faith Was the Mode, Not the Source

When God gave us faith, we believed in Christ and followed him. In following him, we died and rose with him so that God gave us a new righteous spirit made in the image of Jesus. Romans 8:29 says, "For those whom he foreknew he also predestined to be conformed to the image of his Son." God caused us to become righteous because he remade us in the likeness of Christ. However, he made us righteous through the faith he gave us which caused us to believe in Christ and die with him. Our faith served as the instrument through which God would work. Our faith did not make us righteous. God did. God made us righteous *based* on Jesus *through* our faith in him which caused us to follow him.

We see this principle in Ephesians 2:8. This verse distinguishes between the source of our salvation and the mode through which it comes. It says, "For by grace you have been saved through faith." The meaning behind the word "by" is that of source. The phrase "by grace" then means that the grace of God in Christ is the source of our salvation. Moreover, the meaning behind the word "through" is that of a mode of application. The phrase "through faith" then means the mode through which God's grace in Christ is applied to us. The source of our salvation is the grace of Jesus and his death and resurrection. The mode through which we receive it is through faith which causes us to believe in and follow him in his death and resurrection.

Our Status as Chosen Non-Christians

Sometimes we may think about theological issues a little bit off the grid. One of those issues pertains to our status when we as Christians were still non-Christians. Prior to God creating the earth, he had chosen each of us to eventually become righteous based on Christ's work through our faith in him. However, when we were born, God had not given many of us faith yet. He eventually would, but at the time of our birth and even into our childhood, he had not done so yet. We were essentially chosen non-Christians. We were chosen, but we were not yet Christians. The Scriptures, however, do not refer to us as chosen non-Christians or anything explicitly describing our spiritual state. The Scriptures do refer to us with one single special term. They call us *lost*. They refer to us as lost because God had indeed chosen us. We belong to God like a sheep, coin, or son belongs to a person. Because he had chosen us, at some point, he will find[72] us. He does not hope to find us or strive to find us. He will find us. Every

---

[72] This is why the Scriptures speak of lost sheep, not lost wolves.

single person whom God chose, he will eventually find. As lost non-Christians, we may have wandered through difficulties in life or endured countless trials thinking God did not know who we were, but he did. In his discretion, he found us and brought us to Christ.

We each have completed some level of education. After we finished our schooling, we likely began applying for some kind of job. We may have filled out numerous applications or sent out several resumes to different organizations or businesses. Eventually, an individual from one of the organizations called us. This process is not unlike what God did when he gave us faith and brought us to Jesus. At the moment God gave us faith in Jesus, he called us to him.

God Called Us to Jesus

When God called us to Jesus, it followed a hearing of the gospel and occurred simultaneously with God giving us faith. The reason for this is simple. When God called us, he called us to Jesus. God's calling was not a calling to do a certain ministry.[73] God called us to come to Christ and die with him. After we heard about him, God gave us faith, and we believed in him. This sounds a little like what our parents did to us as we grew up. As we played outside on a summer evening, at some point our parents called us inside. When they did this, they got our attention, made us listen to them, and then called us to come inside. God did a similar thing with us when he made us righteous. God gave us faith during a hearing of the gospel and called us non-audibly through the Holy Spirit to follow Jesus. Because of our faith, we obeyed and were no longer lost. This is what the Scriptures refer to as a "holy calling" or the "calling of God." 2 Timothy 1:9 says, "Who saved us and called us with a holy calling."

God Called Us into the Kingdom

When God called us to Jesus, it involved more than a call to be saved from future punishment. God did indeed call us to Jesus so we will not be punished on the Day of Judgment. This in and of itself is grounds for rejoicing and praise. God, however, did more than this. He also called us into his kingdom. This was the content of his preaching. This was the focus of his ministry. When God called us to Jesus, it involved being saved out of this sinful world and into the kingdom of God so we would display

---

[73] There are actually four types of calling in the Scriptures including God calling us to do a certain type of ministry. The first type of calling is his calling us to Christ.

the righteousness of the kingdom. Romans 14:17 says, "For the kingdom of God is not a matter of eating and drinking but of righteousness and peace and joy in the Holy Spirit."

Occasionally, we see religious bumper stickers on cars such as "Try Jesus" or "Got Jesus?" When we see sayings like this we cannot help but wonder if the people realize that our coming to Jesus and entering his righteous kingdom is not something we can do on our own. Our coming to Jesus involved several events that God caused. God was behind these events to bring us to Jesus and into his kingdom. When he did and because he did, something happened to us. What happened to us was not just a lifestyle change or the next fad we would follow. When God brought us to Jesus and into his kingdom, something radically changed within us. The Holy Spirit made us righteous.

Chapter 13

Who the Holy Spirit Is and How He Made Us Righteous

A man once lived in different cities and towns throughout his life. In each of the different places he lived, he enjoyed some pretty good regional food. He lived in Maine and enjoyed the lobster served on the grilled rolls. He lived in Brooklyn and enjoyed the pepperoni pizza served by the slice. After he lived in these places, he moved away and missed a lot of this regional food. So, he decided to attempt to replicate some of these food items in his own kitchen. In doing this, he needed to follow recipes, very specific recipes. Now, he could follow a recipe like most people, but he found that most of the recipes gave a list of ingredients, and only a very brief explanation of when or how to add the ingredients. When he followed them, he ended of producing what looked and smelled like one of those regional dishes, but it did not taste nearly the same. He learned that making good food is about precisely preparing and blending the ingredients together at a specific time and in a specific manner. In a similar way, God made us righteous and placed us into the kingdom so we can glorify him. God, however, did not make us righteous by snapping his fingers. He carefully and lovingly molded us to be who we are so we could glorify him. God did this through the Holy Spirit.

Who the Holy Spirit Is

The name Holy Spirit kind of sounds like it could refer to any spirit that is holy and sanctified, but in this case it does not. The name Holy Spirit refers to one of the three spiritual forms of God. In addition to God the Father and Jesus the Son, the Holy Spirit also exists, and he is also divine like they are. Since the Holy Spirit is a spirit like God the Father, the writers of the Scriptures used names that would not cause confusion between the two. Some of the writers of the Hebrew Old Testament used the Hebrew word *ruach*, which means "breath," "wind," or "spirit" in conjunction with the Hebrew word *Elohim* meaning God. We translate the phrase *ruach elohim* into English as the proper name "Spirit of God." Some of the writers of the Greek New Testament used the Greek word *pnuema*, which also means "breath," "wind," or "spirit" in conjunction with the Greek word *agiov* meaning "holy." We translate the phrase *pnuema agiov* as the proper name "Holy Spirit." In addition to these, the various writers of the Scriptures used different configurations such as "Spirit of the Lord" or "Spirit of Christ," or simply just "Spirit" to describe the Holy Spirit as the third spiritual form of God.

Though the Holy Spirit is divine, he certainly does not exist as an extra. Most of us have been extras at some point in our lives. We may have been involved in a work project with several others. There were certain individuals with the necessary skills assigned to do the main work, and we helped them out when needed. This is not the case with the Holy Spirit. The Holy Spirit is not an extra who helps when God the Father needs him. The Holy Spirit has always existed as God. When God created the earth, God the Father gave the Holy Spirit specific work to do on his behalf.

The Holy Spirit Initially Ruled Us

After God the Father created the heavens and the earth through Jesus, he sent the Holy Spirit to the earth. Genesis 1:2 says, "And the Spirit of God was hovering over the face of the waters." When this verse says that the Spirit of God was hovering over the face of the waters, it means that before God made the earth livable and created Adam and Eve, the Holy Spirit resided on the formless and empty earth. He was there because God would soon make the earth livable and create people to live on it.

When God created people, the Holy Spirit initially ruled over them. Genesis 2:16 says, "And the Lord God commanded the man." The Lord God commanded the man through the Holy Spirit who spoke to him. The Holy Spirit ruled over both Adam and Eve and taught them about how they were to live. He explained to them the various details of what obedience entailed so that they fully knew what God wanted. Most of us have had people rule over us who did not fully explain to us what they wanted, and we were at a loss to know what to do. This was not the case with the Holy Spirit. He knew Adam and Eve and all the people that came from them. He loved them and earnestly desired that they obey God. His goal in teaching them was to help and encourage people to obey God for his glory.

As time went on, the Holy Spirit continued to rule over and teach people directly about how to live. The Holy Spirit instructed Cain and Abel about how to give acceptable offerings to God, though the Scriptures do not explicitly state it. When Cain disobeyed, God rejected his offering. The Holy Spirit, however, spoke to Cain about how to do what is right so Cain knew what was right. Abel, however, obeyed the Holy Spirit's clear instructions about how to obey God, and God accepted his offering. Because of this difference, Cain murdered Abel. Though Cain's actions were an abomination to God, the Holy Spirit did not remain silent, but confronted Cain about it. The Holy Spirit spoke to Cain and advised him of the consequences. The Holy Spirit then sent Cain away, but protected him wherever he would go from anyone who wanted to kill him. The Scriptures do not give all the details, but the Holy Spirit was very active in ruling over people and teaching them about how to live in various circumstances of their lives.

As the Holy Spirit continued speaking to people over the years, their corruption slowly increased. Their corruption did not increase because the Holy Spirit had failed in his job. The Holy Spirit perfectly taught and ruled over people without malice, deceit, or animosity. The corruption of people increased because of the sin within them and their continual refusal to listen to the Spirit. Though the number of people was still relatively small, they all had sin within them, and most of them became more and more corrupt as time went on. As such, the Holy Spirit would not continue speaking with all people directly. Their corruption caused the Holy Spirit to begin to teach and rule over only over his own people.

The Holy Spirit Ruled Over His People by Filling Certain Individuals

Many of us had jobs when we were kids. When we were young, we did our job each day or each week. Most of the time, we did not have trouble. However, on occasion, we would have trouble because we were still young and learning. So, someone such as one of our parents or a friend would come help us. When he did, he would physically come alongside us in his body to help. He was right there with us physically. However, when the Holy Spirit began ruling only his people, it was not quite the same for him. He is a spirit, so he did not physically come alongside in a body in a continuous theophany in the same way that a person comes alongside someone in a body. Instead, he temporarily filled certain individuals to teach and rule his people on his behalf.

The concept of filling someone is pretty much what it sounds like. The Holy Spirit indwelled a person. The Holy Spirit temporarily filled or indwelled a person so he could work through him as he wished. One of the more notable passages early in the Scriptures showing how the Holy Spirit filled someone as a means to rule his people was in the passage pertaining to Joseph. God caused Joseph to be incarcerated in Egypt and filled him with the Holy Spirit. The Holy Spirit temporarily filled Joseph and gave him the ability to interpret dreams. Genesis 41:38 says, "Can we find a man like this, in whom is the Spirit of God?" Joseph then used his ability to interpret a dream Pharaoh had. This led to Pharaoh elevating Joseph to the highest position in Egypt, second only to Pharaoh himself. Through the Holy Spirit, Joseph used his position to save the country from starvation because of a famine. Joseph, however, was not the only person the Holy Spirit filled.

In the course of time, God chose the nation of Israel to foreshadow the future kingdom of God. As such, the Holy Spirit filled or indwelt numerous individuals such as prophets, judges, and kings within Israel. These individuals would teach and rule Israel on the Spirit's behalf and under his direction. As Israel traveled through the wilderness and resided in the Promised Land, the Holy Spirit taught the Israelites about how God the Father wanted them to live. He also warned them about their disobedience throughout their history. Nehemiah 9:30 says, "Many years you bore with them and warned them by your Spirit." The Holy Spirit only filled or indwelt people temporarily because their spirits were inherently sinful. He did not fill them permanently because he had yet not made their spirits inherently righteous. If a person who was temporarily filled with the Spirit sinned, the Holy Spirit could then depart from him. 1 Samuel 16:14 says, "Now the Spirit of the Lord departed from Saul." The Holy Spirit temporarily filled certain people until Jesus arrived.

The Holy Spirit Filled Jesus

In the course of time, Jesus was born on Earth and subsequently began his ministry of establishing the kingdom of God. When he did, the Spirit filled him. Luke 4:1 says, "And Jesus, full of the Holy Spirit, returned from the Jordan and was led by the Spirit." We may not think that Jesus needed to be filled with the Spirit since Jesus was God, but he was. Jesus was not filled because he needed to be, as though he would be less divine if he were not filled. Jesus was filled by the Holy Spirit so that the Holy Spirit worked in unity with him to complete his ministry. In much the same way that the various devices of a computer system work together because they are connected, Jesus established the kingdom of God because he was filled with the Holy Spirit. As the Spirit led Jesus, God the Father had Jesus speak certain words and complete certain works during his ministry of bringing people to himself and into the kingdom of God.

The Holy Spirit Regenerated Us into the Righteous People of the Kingdom

The primary work that Jesus accomplished during his earthly ministry was his death and resurrection. Jesus died because he willingly surrendered his life for us. When God gave us faith and called us to Jesus, we followed Jesus in the likeness of his death. We too willingly surrendered our lives and allowed our spirits to die. We gave them up and did not fight to keep them. When this happened, the Holy Spirit immediately regenerated them and made them into new righteous spirits. John 6:63 says, "It is the Spirit who gives life." We became the new and righteous people of the kingdom of God. As members of the kingdom, we were no longer who we were. We no longer desired to sin and live for our own glory because the Holy Spirit made our spirits into the likeness of Jesus. Romans 8:29 says, "He also predestined to be conformed to the image of his Son." This is what it means for us to be righteous with Christ or have Christ's righteousness.

The Concept of Regeneration

When the Holy Spirit made our spirits new and righteous, the Scriptures call this the "washing of regeneration" or "spiritual baptism"[74] because he cleansed us of our sin. Our naturally sinful spirits died, and the Holy Spirit cleansed them by making them new and righteous. Titus 3:5 says, "He saved us...by the washing of regeneration and renewal of the Holy Spirit." Besides this passage in Titus, the Scriptures do not actually use the term regeneration very much. The Scriptures use other words or phrases to explain the concept of regeneration beginning all the way back in the Old Testament.

When the Old Testament Scriptures spoke about the future regeneration of the Holy Spirit, they used the phrase "new heart." Ezekiel 36:26 says, "And I will give you a new heart, and a new spirit I will put within you." The new heart which they refer to is simply a new spirit. People occasionally refer to non-material entities with physical body parts. They use the metaphor of our right hand to refer to the power we have. They use the metaphor of our spitting something out of our mouths to refer to our rejecting someone. They also use the metaphor of our hearts to refer to our spirits because our spirits give us life similar to our physical hearts. When our old naturally sinful spirits died with Christ, the Holy Spirit gave us new righteous spirits which is the same thing as having regenerated spirits.

---

[74] To baptize an object means to cleanse it.

As we move into the gospel accounts, John spoke of the future regeneration of the Holy Spirit using the phrase "born again." John 3:3 says, "Truly, truly, I say to you, unless one is born again he cannot see the kingdom of God." This is similar to our receiving a new heart, but a little different. When we were physically born, God generated us with a naturally sinful spirit and a naturally sinful body. When we were born again, the Holy Spirit regenerated us with a righteous spirit, even though we still retain a naturally sinful body. Our being born again means we were spiritually born a second time to be righteous.

As we move further into the New Testament epistles, Paul spoke about the regeneration of the Holy Spirit using the phrase "new creation." 2 Corinthians 5:17 says, "If anyone is in Christ, he is a new creation." The word creation here means a creature or object resulting from God's creative actions. When the Holy Spirit regenerated us, he made us new and righteous as the result of his creative actions. He created within us a new heart or new spirit. Our regenerated spirits technically did not exist until the Holy Spirit created them as new spirits.

The Scriptures use these types of words and phrases to refer to the Holy Spirit's regenerating us because we were inherently sinful. We were in our very nature sinful and unrighteous. The Holy Spirit could not indwell us unless he caused a radical change to occur within us so that we became completely new people with new righteous spirits. The Holy Spirit could only make this radical change based on the ministry of Jesus who died and rose to provide us with redemption, cleansing, and forgiveness of sin. Because of Jesus' ministry, the Holy Spirit made us inherently righteous and could fill us permanently.

If we think about this a little bit, we may wonder about those who lived in the Old Testament. They lived prior to Jesus dying and rising, and the Holy Spirit could only fill them temporarily. It seems then that no one was regenerated in the Old Testament, at least not until Jesus died and rose, and the Holy Spirit came on them.

Old Testament Regeneration

The subject of Old Testament regeneration usually involves the main question, "Did the Holy Spirit regenerate people in the Old Testament period?" It is important for us to understand that our regeneration is directly related to Jesus Christ and his placing us into his righteous kingdom. The Holy Spirit could regenerate us because our sinful spirits died and rose with Christ. When they rose, the Holy Spirit remade them as new, righteous spirits in Jesus' likeness. 1 Peter 1:3 says, "He has caused us to be born again to a living hope through the resurrection of Jesus Christ from the dead." Without Christ who died and rose, we could not have died and rose with him. However, Christ did die and rise, and this is reason the Holy Spirit regenerated us. This means the Holy Spirit could not have regenerated those who lived prior to the actual historical death and resurrection of Christ.

There were indeed people in the Old Testament period who God considered righteous. Genesis 6:9 says, "Noah was a righteous man, blameless in his generation." God considered people such as Noah, Abraham, Job, and Daniel righteous because, though their spirits were naturally sinful, they had faith in the one who would make them righteous. Job 19:25 says. "For I know that my Redeemer lives." They lived in their flesh by their faith in the one who would eventually make them righteous in their spirits, but the Holy Spirit had not yet made their spirits righteous. They did not have regenerated spirits until the one they had faith in died and rose from the dead. For this reason, when Jesus died, he went and preached to those who had died prior to his death. He did this so that those among them who had faith could believe, and the Holy Spirit could regenerate their spirits. 1 Peter 4:6 says, "For this is why the gospel was preached even to those who are dead, that though judged in the flesh the way people are, they might live in the spirit the way God does." The Holy Spirit, therefore, only regenerated people after Jesus died and rose from the dead.

God Justifies Those Whom He Made Righteous

Antique dealers buy antiques from people who want to sell them. However, antique dealers often want to know whether a particular antique is genuine. On occasion, the antique dealer will have an expert legitimize the antique and tell him whether the antique is genuine. If the expert establishes that the antique is genuine, the antique dealer can state as a fact that the antique is genuine and better negotiate a price with a seller. When God regenerated us, we became genuinely righteous. We were the real deal when it came to being righteous. God did not simply consider us righteous. God had actually changed us and made us righteous on the inside. We could begin producing the fruit of righteousness in our lives. Because we were genuinely righteous, God then declared us righteous and began treating us righteous. The concept of God declaring us righteous is called "justification."

The word justification in the Old Testament is *tsadeq,* and in the New Testament it is *dikaiosis.* Both words mean "to declare righteous." God declared us righteous because he gave us faith, we died with Christ, and the Holy Spirit regenerated us in

Jesus' likeness to be righteous. Galatians 2:16 says, "We also have believed in Christ Jesus, in order to be justified by faith in Christ." God can declare us righteous because he has the authority to make such a declaration. Romans 3:25-26 says, "This was to show God's righteousness…so that he might be just and the justifier of the one who has faith in Jesus."

Justification does not mean "to make righteous" as some may presume. God's making us righteous is what he did when the Holy Spirit regenerated us. God made us righteous because he remade our naturally sinful spirits in the likeness of Jesus' righteous spirit. Moreover, once he made us righteous, he declared us righteous or justified us. A helpful analogy in understanding this is that of a judge in a courtroom. A judge examines the facts of a person's actions to discover whether he is innocent. If the facts show that the person is innocent, the judge declares the person innocent. The judge's declaration of innocence comes after the facts proving innocence are displayed. The same thing is true with respect to God and our righteousness. God made our spirits righteous by regenerating us in the image of Jesus, though our righteous spirits are left in a sinful body. Since God made us righteous, we are genuinely righteous. He then justifies us and declares us righteous.

Faith and Works

When some of us hear that God declared us righteous because he made us righteous, it makes sense. God gave us faith that caused us to believe in Christ. We followed him and died to our sin. The Holy Spirit regenerated us as righteous people. As a result of all this, we began producing righteous works that proved our righteous states. James 2:24 says, "You see that a person is justified by works and not by faith alone." We only began producing righteous works because of our initial faith in Christ that caused us to become righteous. We could sum up the relationship between our faith and our works as follows; we had faith in Christ, Christ regenerated us into righteous people, we began producing righteous works.

However, for some of us, it is not that clear cut. We are well aware of other Scripture passages that seem to indicate something else. For example, there are passages that speak of our being justified by faith alone, apart from works. Romans 3:28 says, "For we maintain that a man is justified by faith apart from works of the law." We may wonder why this apparent contradiction exists. The truth is it does not exist. We are without a doubt justified by faith alone. Our faith certainly produces righteous works, but we are still justified based on our initial faith in Christ. This verse mentions works, but they are not the works that *result* from our faith in Christ as Christians. They are a different kind of works. They are works a non-Christian does to try to show God that he is righteous so God will declare him righteous. To understand this, it is important to realize that implied in the verse is a comparison of two types of people.

Romans 3:28 implies that one person has faith in Jesus. His faith is a genuine faith, and it is all he has. He has faith alone. He believed in Christ and died with him. The Holy Spirit regenerated him to have a new, righteous spirit so he can produce the fruit of righteousness. God then declared him righteous because of his initial faith. He was the textbook definition of someone who God justified by faith alone. The second person, however, is nothing like him.

Romans 3:28 also implies that another person does not have faith. He does not believe in Christ, and if he were to hear about Christ, he would by no means follow him and surrender his life. However, he knows that a time will come when sinners in the world will be punished for their sin, and the righteous in the kingdom of God will be saved. He also knows that for God to transfer him from this sinful world to this perfectly righteous kingdom, he must become righteous and engage in righteous works. If he does not, he will not enter it, and he will not be saved from the destiny of the sinful world. So, he analyzes his life and attempts to do righteous works on his own and get God to declare him righteous. In his mind, if he can just live the right way on his own, he can get God to declare him righteous, and get a ticket into the kingdom. God, however, will not. God will not declare righteous any naturally sinful person who attempts to produce the fruit of righteousness by doing good works. Romans 3:20 says, "For by works of the law no human being will be justified in his sight."

This man does not have faith and cannot produce righteous works. However, he tries to perform righteous works on his own. These are the works Romans 3:28 refers to when it says, "apart from works." God, however, justifies us because we have faith. He will never justify a non-Christian who attempts to be righteous on his own. Our faith causes us to follow Jesus, and the Holy Spirit regenerates us into righteous people.

Regenerated Christians are Truly Righteous

Nice restaurants in major cities often have valets. Whenever a patron of the restaurant would come to the restaurant, he would stop his car in front of the restaurant, and the valet would park the car. On one occasion, at a restaurant in a particular city, a man and his wife pulled up in a very nice luxury car. When the man gave the valet the keys, he told him there was a smell coming from the engine, but not to worry about it. Not thinking much about it, the valet then parked the car, and the man and his wife went into restaurant. When the valet got out of the car, he noticed a spot on the hood, and it was turning color. He waited a minute, and then smoke started coming out from under the hood. He waited a little bit more, and then flames started coming out. He then ran into the restaurant and called the fire department. When the fire department showed up, the engine compartment of this beautiful luxury car was engulfed in flames. Now, when the fire department puts out a fire inside an engine compartment, they do not open the driver's door and pop the latch. They use hydraulic tools, rip the hood open, and stick the hose in.

While the fire department was putting the fire out, the valet's supervisor comes out to see what is going on. He looks at the valet and asks him what had happened. The valet told him he did not know, and that the car just caught on fire. The supervisor ran back in, found the man who owned the car, and they both came out. The man was obviously shaken seeing his car on fire with the hood ripped open. The supervisor resumed questioning the valet about what happened. However, at this point the man spoke up. He told the supervisor that it was not the valet's fault because he had had a problem with the car before he gave it to the valet. The valet was relieved to say the least. The man could have remained silent or could have just lied, and the valet would have been to blame, and the restaurant would have paid. However, he did not. He was righteous.

We as Christians are righteous. We are not just considered righteous. We are righteous because the Holy Spirit remade our spirits to be righteous in the likeness of Christ. Like Christ, we thirst for righteousness and seek to have its demands met. Like Christ, we are drawn to live righteously in our lives and have joy in seeing others live righteously. The mere thought of unrighteousness makes us uncomfortable, uneasy, and at times even sick. As righteous people we want to live as righteous people within the righteous kingdom of God. We have a problem though. We do not always live righteously. This is serious issue. The Holy Spirit made us righteous, and we have a righteous spirit, but we have a struggle to live righteously. Because of this, when the Holy Spirit made us righteous, he sanctified and indwelt us.

Chapter 14

What the Holy Spirit Did After He Made Us Righteous

    Some of us have keen eyes when it comes to buying items for our homes. When we need a special item such as a piece of furniture to perfectly accent a room, we look carefully for the right one. We usually want one that has an inherent high quality and is well made. We have learned, however, that finding items of an inherent high quality can be difficult. We cannot simply drive to a local store and find what we are looking for. Instead, we have to search the internet or antique stores. When we do find what we are looking for, it may be in poor shape and disrepair. It may be damaged, corroded, and its patina is far beyond what we consider part of its character. However, this does not dissuade us from acquiring it because we know that under the grit and scuffs is an item of inherent high quality. We know that after we restore it, it will be useful to us as a means to glorify and beautify our homes.

    The same thing is true with respect to the Holy Spirit and us. We were born naturally sinful and damaged to the extent that we did not glorify God. People may have considered our lives honorable as they saw how we lived. However, as soon as they scratched the surface and spend some time with us, they saw an ugly, sinful, and disobedient person. As sinful people, God destined to destroy us. No one could really question God's doing this. We ourselves throw out moldy food, replace worn tires, and discard broken glass. God our creator can certainly destroy us for being sinful and failing to glorify him. God, however, did not. The Holy Spirit regenerated us from being sinful to being righteous. He took us out of the sinful world destined for destruction and placed us into the righteous and eternal kingdom of God. In doing this, the Holy Spirit set us apart so that we are useful to God for the purpose of glorifying him. The work that the Holy Spirit did in setting us apart for this purpose is called sanctification.

The Holy Spirit Sanctified Us

When the Holy Spirit regenerated us, he made our spirits righteous in the likeness of Jesus. However, it was not enough for God just to make us righteous and leave it at that. He would do more than that because our being righteous required another step. At the moment when God made us righteous, he also sanctified us. The word "sanctify" is based on the Hebrew word *qadash* and the Greek word *hagiazo*, both of which mean "to set apart for God's purpose." "Sanctify" does not mean to simply "set apart" because we can set apart many things that do not pertain to God. We can set apart some money to use toward a new roof. We can set apart some clothes to donate to a charity. "To sanctify" means to set apart *for God's purpose*. The Holy Spirit *made* us righteous and then set us apart from the sinful world to *live* righteously so we glorify God, which the world did not do. 2 Timothy 2:21 says, "If anyone cleanses himself from what is dishonorable, he will be a vessel for honorable use, set apart as holy, useful to the master of the house, ready for every good work." Because the Holy Spirit sanctified us, he made us holy. We can then be called holy ones or saints as opposed to sinners.[75]

We Are Holy Because Jesus Is Holy

The Holy Spirit's making us holy was directly connected to his regenerating us in the likeness of Jesus. Hebrews 9:14 says, "How much more will the blood of Christ, who through the eternal Spirit offered himself without blemish to God, purify our conscience from dead works to serve the living God." The word "to" in this verse indicates the purpose for Christ's offering himself on the cross. Christ offered himself so we could become righteous and serve God by engaging in good works. We cannot be righteous and serve God without Christ.

The Scriptures explain how God sanctified us through Christ using the two analogies of leavening and grafting. Romans 11:16 says, "If the dough offered as first fruits is holy, so is the whole lump, and if the root is holy, so are the branches." In this verse, there are two brief analogies. One pertains to leaven within a piece of dough, and one pertains to branches from a root. Regarding the dough, in the leavening process a person places a small piece of leavened dough within a larger lump of unleavened dough. The leaven from the piece of leavened dough permeates into the lump of unleavened dough until the entire lump is made leavened. In a similar way regarding

---

[75] A sinner is someone who is still naturally sinful. A saint or holy one is someone who God has sanctified and made holy. The Scriptures never call Christians sinners.

the root, in the grafting process a person takes a branch and attaches it to a root. The sap of the root begins spreading into the branch to give it life. These two metaphors show that Jesus is the piece of leavened dough and the sap-filled root. When the Holy Spirit makes us righteous in the likeness of Christ, he gives Christ's holiness to us who are the unleavened lump and the branches, respectively. Because of Christ, we are no longer naturally sinful, but holy and sanctified.

Some of us grew up hearing that our sanctification was a process. As we became sanctified, there were a series of actions, some that God did and some that we did. When we heard this, we may have just accepted it even though we did not really understand what the process entailed. However, as we studied the Scriptures, they seemed to teach that sanctification was also a one-time event based on Jesus' death and resurrection. This may have caused a dilemma for us that made us wonder whether sanctification was a one-time event or a process. It is both.

The Sanctification of Our Spirits

When Jesus died and rose from the dead, he sanctified our spirits. Jesus' death and resurrection was a one-time act, and it sanctified us permanently. Hebrews 10:10-14 says, "And by that will we have been sanctified through the offering of the body of Jesus Christ once for all." When we think about this, however, we realize that we still sin. We can live to glorify God, but we do not always do so because we still sin. The reason for this is that the Holy Spirit sanctified our spirits once and for all, but not our bodies. Our bodies still contain sin. They did not die with Christ, and the Holy Spirit did not regenerate them. They have not been sanctified. However, the Holy Spirit will work with us so that our bodies will gradually become sanctified. Because of his work, we will eventually become sanctified in both spirit and body. 1 Thessalonians 5:23 says, "Now the God peace himself sanctify you completely, and may your whole spirit and soul and body be kept blameless at the coming of our Lord Jesus Christ." The Holy Spirit sanctifies our bodies by teaching us how to live in them.

The Sanctification of Our Bodies

If we are to live as sanctified spirits within naturally sinful bodies, it will entail hard work. It will entail denial, deprivation, and pain each day. Living as sanctified people means we must strive to live righteously instead of sinfully. Romans 6:19 says, "For just as you once presented your members as slaves to impurity and to lawlessness leading to more lawlessness, so now present your members as slaves to righteousness, leading to sanctification [holiness]." However, we cannot strive to live holy lives by listening to our own wisdom and relying on our own will power. It is important that we listen to exactly what the Holy Spirit teaches us to do and rely on the power he provides. The Holy Spirit will give us all the information we need and the power to do what he says in every circumstance that requires holiness. As the Holy Spirit does this, we can live in our bodies in accordance with our sanctified spirits. 1 Thessalonians 4:1-4 says, "That as you received from us how you ought to walk and to please God…For you know what instructions we gave you through the Lord Jesus. For this is the will of God, your sanctification…that each one of you know how to control his own body in holiness." As we strive to live as sanctified spirits in our naturally sinful bodies, we will be able to please the Lord in everything we do and produce the fruit of righteousness.

This does not sound as clean cut as we might think. Many of us go to work, school, family gatherings, where we are influenced to sin. As we are influenced, we realize that sometimes the Holy Spirit does not teach us how to live righteously around sinful people. Instead, he teaches us to avoid them. Some of us who work or live around non-Christians understand this based on personal experience. The non-Christians we live around will engage in sinful activities and conversations. It is their nature to do this. As Christians, we know when they will do this or are about to. In these cases, the Holy Spirit does not teach us to remain with them and painfully resist sinning. Rather, he teaches us to separate from them.

Living in Sanctified Bodies May Mean Separation

In order for us to live successfully as holy people, in many cases we must separate ourselves from the sinful beliefs and practices of others, whether Christians or non-Christians. Isaiah 52:11 says, "Depart, depart, go out from there; touch no unclean thing; go out from the midst of her; purify yourselves." The Holy Spirit originally applied this passage to the Israelites who were departing from Babylon. He told them not to follow the sinful beliefs and practices of their old masters after they left. The Holy Spirit reapplied this passage to the Corinthian Christians in 2 Corinthians 6:17. He told them not to be unequally yoked to non-Christians. However, it is also applicable to all of us. It means we should separate ourselves from non-Christians or even Christians so that we do not to allow their sinful beliefs and practices to influence us and cause us to sin.

Separating ourselves though does not mean we isolate ourselves. When God sanctified our spirits, he also left us in a world of unsanctified non-Christians, but this was his will. God left us here to fulfill earthly responsibilities pertaining to family and work. He also left us here to fulfill spiritual responsibilities pertaining to ministry. God did not intend for us to isolate ourselves. So, as we live among ungodly people, we fulfill our earthly and spiritual responsibilities. However, at the same time we prevent ourselves from being influenced or forced to participate in their sinful beliefs and practices.

God Will Cleanse and Forgive Us When We Sin in Our Naturally Sinful Bodies

Even as we strive to live as sanctified spirits within naturally sinful bodies, we will still sin. God caused us to be sanctified in our spirits, but he also allows us to sin in our bodies. For this reason, God provides cleansing and forgiveness for us when we do sin. John 13:10 says, "Jesus answered, 'Those who have had a bath need only to wash their feet; their whole body is clean.'" When we do sin, we can present ourselves to God and sincerely request to be cleansed and forgiven. 1 John 1:9 says, "If we confess our sins, he is faithful and just to forgive us our sins and to cleanse us from all unrighteousness." Implied within the word "confess" is the concept of sincerity. When we confess our sin, we are sincerely telling God we sinned and sincerely asking him to cleanse and forgive us. The verse does not say "vocalize." This would mean that we simply tell God the fact that we sinned and ask for cleansing and forgiveness without any regard to an internal motive of brokenness and desire to repent. God, however, will indeed cleanse and forgive us when we sin, but it must be based on our sincere request to repent so we can glorify God.

The Holy Spirt Indwells Us as Sanctified People

As Christians, it is important that we constantly separate ourselves from the sinful beliefs and practices of others. The Holy Spirit's sanctifying us to be holy is not a status we should take lightly. The Holy Spirit sanctified us because we are God's temple, and he indwells us. We are similar to the temple in the Old Testament. In the Old Testament, the temple was holy, and the Holy Spirit's presence dwelt in it. Exodus 29:44 says, "I will consecrate the tent of meeting and the altar. Aaron also and his sons I will consecrate to serve me as priests. I will dwell among the people of Israel and will be their God." God, however, designed the Old Testament temple to be temporary and be replaced by the eternal temple of Christ and his body. We are Christ's body and his eternal temple. Through us as the eternal holy temple of Christ, God displays his righteousness. 1 Corinthians 3:16-17 says, "Do you not know that you are God's temple and that God's spirit dwells in you?...For God's temple is holy, and you are that temple." Unlike the earthly temple, the Holy Spirit has sanctified us forever and will dwell within us forever.

The Holy Spirit Permanently Indwelled or Filled Us

After Jesus died, rose, and ascended to Heaven, the Holy Spirit went with him. God, however, sent the Holy Spirit back to Earth to permanently dwell within those who believed in Jesus and who he had made righteous. As the Holy Spirit permanently dwelled within his people, he taught them everything God wanted them to know about how to live as his righteous people within the kingdom of God. John 16:13 says, "When the Spirit of truth comes, he will guide you into all the truth, for he will not speak on his own authority, but whatever he hears [from God the Father] he will speak, and he will declare to you the things what are to come." The Spirit in this verse is the Holy Spirit who is doing God's work of revealing the truth.

When the Holy Spirit came and indwelt the first Christians, it was not really new. We may read Acts 2 and think that it was the first time the Holy Spirit indwelt people, but it was not. The Holy Spirit had indwelt people before, but it was only temporary. The Holy Spirit indwelt Joseph in Egypt, Saul in Israel, and Daniel in Babylon as well as many other people. When the Holy Spirit came in Acts 2, he came to permanently indwell people. Centuries earlier, the prophet Joel had spoken about God's sending the Holy Spirit to permanently indwell his people. Joel 2:28 says, "I will pour out my Spirit on all flesh." Fifty days after Jesus' resurrection, God the Father sent the Holy Spirit from Heaven at the request of Jesus to permanently dwell within anyone whom the Holy Spirit had made righteous including the apostles.

After this initially happened, the Holy Spirit would also permanently indwell anyone who he had made righteous. When Peter preached the gospel on the Day of Pentecost, three thousand people believed and the Holy Spirit began dwelling within them permanently. Acts 2:38-41 says, "Repent and be baptized every one of you in the name of Jesus Christ for the forgiveness of your sins, and you will receive the gift of the Holy Spirit...there were added that day about three thousand souls." Even after the Day of Pentecost, with the exception of two instances, nothing has changed. When the Holy Spirit made any of us righteous, regardless of where we live in the world, he began to indwell us permanently.

When the Scriptures speak of the Holy Spirit's dwelling within us, they do not always refer to it with the phrase "dwelling within." Sometimes the Scriptures refer to it as "filling." The Scripture's use of two different words to explain the same event raises the question of whether the concept of dwelling within is actually the same as the concept of filling. Opinions on this issue vary. Some of us believe our being filled with the Holy Spirit means he controls us. This is distinct from his dwelling within us, which simply means he lives within us. If this distinction is correct, it means that the Holy Spirit will always dwell within us, but he may not always fill or control us. The Scriptures, however, do not teach this.

If we review New Testament passages, we will find that the Holy Spirit's filling us and his dwelling within us refer to the same act. The phrases "filled with the Holy Spirit" and "the Holy Spirit dwells within" are simply different ways we use language to explain this particular activity of the Holy Spirit. The Scriptures do use the word "filling" or one of its cognates predominantly, but they also use other words and phrases such as "come on," "receive," and "pour on" to express the concept that the Holy Spirit dwells us.

We can see that this is true fairly easily. As we review the Scriptures, they never explain that we can be indwelt by the Holy Spirit, but not filled with him. The Scriptures would certainly elaborate on a concept as important as this. If we could be permanently indwelt by the Holy Spirit, but not filled or controlled by him, the Scriptures would explain or at the least mention it, but they do not. We can also see that the Holy Spirit's filling and his indwelling are the same thing in the fact that on some occasions, when the Scriptures clearly show a situation when the Holy Spirit indwelt his people, they used the word filled. For example, Acts 4:31 says, "The place in which they were gathered together was shaken, and they were all filled with the Holy Spirit." In this passage, the Holy Spirit began to indwell the Christians, even though the verse uses the word "filled." So, the phrases "filling of the Holy Spirit" and the "indwelling of the Holy Spirit" mean the same thing.

The Holy Spirit Indwelled Us Immediately, With Two Historical Exceptions

We are all fairly accustomed to the view that when we each became a Christian, the Holy Spirit entered into us and began indwelling us. This has been true for all of us Christians throughout history. As we trace the spiritual heritage of the church back through the centuries, this characteristic is common to all Christians in all regions of the earth. As we continue back to the first Christians mentioned in Acts 2, we see that the Holy Spirit immediately indwelt them when they believed in Christ. However, as we trace this back, we will also see that, historically, there were two exceptions to this.

God had for centuries worked with the Jewish people. People over all the earth connected the reputation, the circumstances, and well-being of the Jewish people to God. When Jesus came to earth, he predominantly ministered to them. Logically then, the first Christians the Holy Spirit indwelt were Jews. However, God would not work exclusively with the Jews. He would also work with non-Jews. So, the first time the Holy Spirit dwelt within Samaritan[76] Christians and Gentile[77] Christians, he did so a little differently, but for good reason.

According to Acts 8, the first Samaritan Christians believed in Jesus when Philip went to Samaria and preached the gospel. Acts 8:12 says, "When they believed Philip as he preached the good news about the kingdom of God and the name of Jesus Christ, they were baptized." When Philip preached the gospel, however, they had not yet received the Holy Spirit. Philip then left, and later Peter and John arrived. When Peter and John laid their hands on the Samaritan Christians, they received the Holy Spirit. Acts 8:14-15 says, "They sent to them Peter and John, who came down and prayed for them that they might receive the Holy Spirit." The Samaritans did not immediately receive the Holy Spirit when they believed, but had to wait until the apostles prayed for them and laid their hands on them.

A very similar thing happened to some of the first Gentile Christians as recorded in Acts 19. In this passage, the apostle Paul is in Ephesus. He finds some Gentiles who were followers of the law and of John's ministry. These Gentiles, however, had not yet heard about Jesus. In Acts 19:3, Paul says, "Into what then were you baptized? They said, "Into John's baptism." Paul then preached the gospel to them, and they believed. It was not until moments later when Paul laid his hands on them that they received the Holy Spirit. Acts 19:6 says, "And when Paul had laid his hands on them, the Holy Spirit came on them." The Gentiles did not immediately receive the Holy Spirit when they believed, but had to wait until Paul laid his hands on them.

God delayed giving the Holy Spirit in these two instances so that he could specifically show that the Samaritans and Gentiles were also partakers of the gospel and the Holy Spirit, as well as the Jews. Up until these two instances, most of the people who had believed were Jewish. God delayed giving the Holy Spirit to both the

---

[76] "Samaritan" means *watcher* [of the Torah]. Samaritans descended from the original tribes of Israel, but they worshipped God at a different location in Israel than the Jews who worshipped in the correct location, Jerusalem.

[77] "Gentile" is an English transliteration of the Latin word *gentillis* meaning "peoples." Translators of the Scriptures used it to translate the Hebrew word *goy* and Greek word *ethnos*. It refers to people who are not Jewish.

Samaritans and the Gentiles so he could show others that non-Jews were acceptable to him. God specifically showed the Samaritans and Gentiles were acceptable by having the apostles lay their hands on them as they received the Holy Spirit. The laying on of hands signified that one thing was acceptable to God. When the Jewish apostles, who had God's authority, gave the Holy Spirit to non-Jews through laying their hands on them, they were signifying that non-Jews were also acceptable to God and were also recipients of the Holy Spirit.

The Holy Spirit Does Not Undo His Work in Us

Historically, whenever someone wanted to protect something he owned, he often used a seal of some kind. If he wanted to protect his valuables within a container such as a box, he would seal the container with tape. A seal was something on a container or scroll that substantially prevented someone besides the rightful person from having access to the contents. We see this with Pilate and Jesus' tomb. In Matthew 27:64-66, Pilate ordered that the soldiers seal Jesus' tomb so his disciples could not steal his body. The seal on Jesus' tomb was not just the rock itself which could be rolled. It was something that would substantially prevent anyone from rolling the rock away and accessing the tomb.

When the Holy Spirit regenerated us, sanctified us, and began to indwell us, it was permanent. For those who lived prior to Jesus, if they sinned, the Holy Spirit may have left them. With us, he will not. He will not desecrate us and leave us even though we sin. The Holy Spirit will remain with us forever as his people in the kingdom of God. Because of this, when the Holy Spirit began to permanently indwell us, he became a seal. 2 Corinthians 1:21-22 says, "And it is God…who has also put his seal on us and given us his Spirit in our hearts as a guarantee." The Holy Spirit's presence within us, as opposed to a seal outside a box, protects us and preserves the work God had done. Like the Israelites who the Holy Spirit protected and preserved as a cloud by day and fire by night, the Holy Spirit protects and preserves us so God will establish us on the earth in the kingdom of God.

This very issue pertains to one of the more popular questions people ask regarding God and theology in general. They want to know whether we as Christians can fall away. They may ask the question a little differently such as "Can I lose my faith?" or "Can I fall away from Christ?" Regardless of the wording, the issue is the same. They want to know whether we will retain our faith in Christ and persevere in the kingdom. This concept pertains to the subject of perseverance or eternal security.

God Causes Us to Persevere as Christians

Some of us may argue for hours over the issue of whether we can lose our faith, fall away from Christ, and be removed from the kingdom of God. Others of us may lose sleep thinking about it. The truth is, however, that we will not. God began working in us to make us perfect, and will complete in us the work he started. He will keep us in the kingdom of God, and eventually give us the earth as our inheritance with Christ. Philippians 1:6 says, "And I am sure of this, that he who began a good work in you will bring it to completion." God will not remove our faith, unregenerate us, or remove the Holy Spirit from dwelling within us. God will not be like a builder who builds a house and after he is half done, begins tearing it down.

The fact that we sin, however, does not change things. We sin, and there are sins we do regularly and flagrantly. As we struggle to overcome our sin, we sometimes lose the struggle, and God may discipline us. When God disciplines us, he imposes on us circumstances that cause discomfort and pain to a certain degree. We feel God's discipline, and it is uncomfortable. It is supposed to be. However, our experiencing God's discipline does not mean he retracted our faith in Christ or removed us from the kingdom of God. If we think about it, the opposite is actually true. The presence of God's discipline shows us that we indeed have faith, and that it is real. 1 Peter 1:3-7 says, "He has caused us to be born again to a living hope through the resurrection of Jesus Christ from the dead, to an inheritance that is imperishable, undefiled, and unfading, kept in heaven for you…*so that the tested genuineness of your faith*…may be found to result in praise and glory and honor." The presence of God's discipline, even if severe, does not indicate that we lost our faith. It actually indicates that we have faith because God is working in our lives as his children within his righteous kingdom to bring about some change so that we become more righteous and glorify him.

For some of us, this may be encouraging. To others, their feelings about God's discipline does not overpower their thinking about the Scriptures. They read and try to interpret certain verses that seem to indicate that we can lose our faith. One of those is Hebrews 6:4-6 which says, "In the case of those who have once been enlightened, and have tasted the heavenly gift, and have shared in the Holy Spirit, and have tasted the goodness of the word of God…and then have fallen away." At first, these verses seem to indicate that God may remove our faith and cause us to fall away, but they do not.

In this passage, the people whom the Spirit mentions are not genuine Christians. They are non-Christians who have heard the gospel, but have not believed it. The Holy Spirit has caused them to hear about Jesus and the kingdom of God, but they rejected it. For this reason, the passage uses words like, "taste" and "enlightened." These words indicate that the non-Christians heard the gospel, and they considered it, but they never actually believed it. This makes sense when we realize that many people throughout history have heard about Jesus and his kingdom, but did not believe in him.

A helpful analogy in understanding this is that of a food sampling kiosk. When we go to the grocery store, we occasionally see a store employee at a kiosk offering food to shoppers for them to sample. Shoppers occasionally walk up and taste the food offered to them. They consider buying it for a meal, but most of them do not. In the same way, non-Christians hear the gospel, and they consider it. They are essentially tasting the gospel and partaking of the Holy Spirit's teaching or words. However, many of them do not believe it. This is what Hebrews 6:4-6 is teaching.

God Gives Us Hope

When a person wonders whether he can lose his faith and fall away from the kingdom, it may reveal a deeper issue than just how he feels about God's discipline or how he interprets a Bible verse. It may reveal a deeper issue because we as genuine Christians have a solid expectation that we will persevere within the kingdom and receive the inheritance of the earth. We know it like we know our own names. It is part of who we are. We have this expectation because it is not something we believe on our own. We cannot force ourselves to believe we will persevere any more than a soldier sitting in a helicopter flying to the frontline of a war can force himself to believe he will survive. We have a firm and solid expectation that we will preserve because God himself gave it to us. This expectation is called "hope."

When God gives us hope we begin to know for certain that we will preserve to the end and not fall away from the kingdom. We expect to arrive at the judgment and for God to find us righteous because of Christ. We expect to receive the inheritance of the earth as members of the kingdom of God. 1 Peter 1:3-4 says, "According to his great mercy, he has caused us to be born again to a living hope through the resurrection of Jesus Christ from the dead." We know we will persevere and we expect to.

This meaning of hope may be different than what some of us understand hope to be. Some may believe that if we hope for something, we wish to receive it. We may say that we hope it does not rain, meaning that we wish it will not rain. This difference is important. When God gives us hope that we will persevere and not fall away, we do not just wish this happens. It will happen. It is firm. It cannot be changed or altered, even by us. God will cause us to persevere, and gives us a firm expectation that we will.

Ephesians 1:18 says, "That you may know what is the hope to which he has called you, what are the riches of his glorious inheritance in [for] the saints."

God Gives Us Glorified Bodies

As we live with our hope, we live with a seeming paradox. We know we will persevere, but we also know we will die. When God regenerated us, he only regenerated our spirits, not our bodies. We are essentially righteous spirits housed within sinful bodies within the kingdom of God. Our righteous spirits will persevere, but our sinful bodies will not. They will one day come to an end. Though we work with the Holy Spirit to make and even buffet our bodies to be righteous, God still made them naturally sinful, and they must die. However, along with our hope that God will keep us in the kingdom and give us the earth, we also have hope that he will give us new righteous bodies. Our hope informs us that when God resurrects us at the first resurrection, he will give us new righteous bodies for our righteous spirits to live within. 1 Corinthians 15:19-22 says, "If in Christ we have hope in this life only, we are of all people most to be pitied. But in fact Christ has been raised from the dead…in Christ shall all be made alive."

Our resurrected bodies will be different in composition than our earthly bodies. Our naturally sinful earthly bodies are designed for the current earth and its conditions. We can live on the current earth because God designed our bodies to blend in with the earthly environment. Our righteous heavenly bodies, however, will be designed for the new earth and its conditions. We will be able to live on the new earth because God will design our bodies to blend in with the new earth's environment. Because of these two main differences, our heavenly bodies will be composed of a different kind of flesh that is not subject to decay or death. 1 Corinthians 15:39-42 says, "For not all flesh is the same…There are heavenly bodies and earthly bodies…So is it with the resurrection of the dead. What is sown is perishable; what is raised is imperishable." Because our bodies will be heavenly and righteous, they will be glorified bodies which means they will be exalted and honorable.

When we were young, we all knew what it meant to quit. We played on teams, joined various school groups, or engaged in personal projects. We experienced moments when things got hard or we got discouraged, and we thought about how easy our lives would be if we just quit. It was the easy way for us to get out of a commitment, and we all likely did quit some things. However, when it comes to God and his work in our lives, the thought of quitting has never crossed his mind. He initially chose us long before he made us, and he has never thought about letting us go. Even when we sin or purposely chose to disobey, he does not abandon us. He made us righteous and brought us into his kingdom through Jesus Christ. He will continue to work in our lives so that we become more and more righteous in how we live until he finally establishes us as his kingdom on the earth. There is nothing we can do to get God to stop his work in us. Though we fail, disobey, and even outright rebel, God will faithfully complete his work in us, and it will be glorious. 2 Timothy 2:13 says, "If we are faithless, he remains faithful – for he cannot deny himself."

Michael Jones

Entering the Kingdom

Chapter 15

How Christ's Righteousness Causes Us to Glorify God

There are usually many things wrong with a dysfunctional company. It contains mismanaged staff, mishandled resources, and misallocated money. As a result of the company's numerous dysfunctions, it loses customers as well as the necessary money it needs to remain viable. Left unchanged, it will eventually dissolve. Companies like this are not uncommon. However, in one of these companies, a man may go in and change things. He replaces unproductive and non-efficient staff. He modifies policy and procedures. He completely reorganizes how the company functions. As a result of his work, the company gains customers and increases profits. The company may still exist within the same building and on the same property, but it is a completely different company. It has begun to have a reputation of providing quality products, taking care of its employees, and giving back to the community of which it is part.

In a similar way, we were born naturally sinful. We followed our own natural passions to sin. We thought sinful thoughts, spoke sinful words, and engaged in sinful works. We were unproductive at bringing glory to God and lived only for our own. Left unchanged, God would have eventually destroyed us. However, according to God's good pleasure, he transformed us on the inside. The Holy Spirit gave us Christ's righteousness which replaced our natural sinfulness. Christ's righteousness was not just a standard he enlightened our minds to follow. It was a standard the Spirit gave us and wrote on our hearts. We had Christ's righteousness within us, and we thirsted and hungered to practice it. We *were* righteous because we *had* Christ's righteousness.

What Jesus' Righteousness Does Within Us

Having Christ's righteousness means we have a righteous spirit within us that is naturally inclined to do what is right. The word righteousness is based on the Hebrew word *tsedaqah* and the Greek word *dikaiosune*, both of which mean "in accordance with what is right, proper and honorable." We can display righteousness in our lives, which we could not do before because it is not our righteousness, but Christ's. Philippians 3:9 says, "Not having a righteousness of my own...but that which comes through faith in Christ, the righteousness from God that depends on faith." Christ's righteousness then produces fruit in our lives. Philippians 1:11 says, "Filled with the fruit of righteousness that comes through Jesus Christ, to the glory and praise of God." The fruit of Christ's righteousness produces within us certain godly qualities characteristic of a person in the kingdom of God. These qualities define who we are, and their genuine presence within us indicates that we are indeed part of the kingdom of God. There are numerous qualities that Christ's righteousness produces in us. The first one is love.

Christ's Righteousness Produces Love in Us

When the Holy Spirit gave us Christ's righteousness, it produced God's love within us. In the Old Testament, the English word love is based on the Hebrew word *ahav* and its variations. In the New Testament, the English word love is based on the Greek words *agapae* and *phileo* and their variations.[78] Our having God's love within us means we have an interest in what God has an interest in. God has an interest in his people living righteously and glorifying him. He gives them their basic needs as well as providing them with their spiritual needs so they can do this. When we have God's love within us, it causes us to be devoted to God and seek these interests for other people. We want for them what God wants for them.

When we were in our naturally sinful states, we were outside of the kingdom of God. We did not have Christ's righteousness, and God's love was not within us. We had worldly love in our hearts that caused us to only glorify ourselves. When the Scriptures describe a person who only loves himself, they speak about the things that he uses to glorify himself.[79] They speak about a person loving the world or the things in the world because it is through these things that he can receive pleasure and glory for himself. 1 John 2:15-17 says, "Do not love the world or the things in the world...For all that is in the world - the desires of the flesh and the desires of the eyes and pride of life - is not from the Father but is from the world." This verse implies that when we were naturally

---

[78] There are other words for love in Greek such as *eros* in ancient Greek and *storgae* in Modern Greek, but they are never used in the New Testament.

[79] This can be seen in the kinds of things people pursue. For example, people pursue the kinds of jobs, the kinds of possessions, and the kinds of spouses that will give them glory.

sinful, we loved the things of the world of which we were part so we could obtain pleasure and glory for ourselves.

However, having received Christ's righteousness, we have the quality of God's love which is a noun, a verb, and an object. God's love as a noun begins within our hearts. God placed his love within our hearts when he made us righteous and gave us the Holy Spirit. Romans 5:5 says, "God's love has been poured into our hearts through the Holy Spirit who has been given to us." It is necessary that we have God's love in our hearts so that we can love others in our actions.

Once God's love is within our hearts, we can show love as a verb toward others. John 15:12 says, "This is my commandment, that you love one another as I have loved you." If we have God's love within us, then we will have an interest in treating people as God would treat them so he is glorified. Showing love toward others does not mean giving people what brings glory to themselves. If we give a rich person more money, an overweight person more food, or a child any toy he wants, this is not love. These things do not bring glory to God, and God has no interest in giving these things to them. God does, however, have an interest in giving things to people that are conducive to his glory.

Those who receive God's love from us become the objects of his and our love. We call these people "our love" or "our beloved." Our having God's love within us and showing it toward another person helps them to glorify God. A second quality Christ's righteousness produces in us is joy.

Christ's Righteousness Produces Joy in Us

When the Holy Spirit gave us Christ's righteousness, it produced joy within us. Joy is a pleasure that God puts within us from our having obtained something conducive to our well-being. The English word joy is based on the Hebrew word *simchah* and the Greek work *chara*, both of which carry this meaning. A common synonym for joy is happiness, but the word joy is predominantly used in the Scriptures.[80] When we think of joy, we may think about how we feel at certain times. We are joyful because we had a child, or we are joyful because we are going on vacation. Joy, however, is much more than just an emotion. It is a pleasure that God gives us.

When we were in our naturally sinful states and outside the kingdom, God did not give us joy or pleasure. God did not want us to have joy for sinning. As a result, we

---

[80] This is the reason for the infrequent use of the word happiness in both the Old and New Testaments.

sought our own joy by obtaining things within the world for our own glory. We sought and pursued things which we perceived would bring us joy. For example, we may have wanted to feel better about ourselves so we degraded another person. However, our obtaining things by sinning only provided us a temporal kind of joy. This kind of joy did not last, and only pleased us for a moment. Job 20:5 says, "The exulting of the wicked is short, and the joy of the godless but for a moment?"

However, when the Holy Spirit made us righteous and placed us within the kingdom, he gave us joy. He did not just make us happy or smile. He gave us a genuine joy. The Scriptures call this kind of joy the "joy of the Lord." Nehemiah 8:10 says, "The joy of the Lord is your strength." God gave us the joy of the Lord because we live for the purpose of glorifying him. The more we display Christ's righteousness, and the more we glorify God, the more joy he gives us. The degree to which we glorify God corresponds to the amount of joy we have. John 15:11 says, "These things I have spoken to you so that my joy may be in you, and that your joy may be made full." As God works in our lives, it may be painful at times because we go through trials and tests. However, the trials cause us to glorify God, and as we do so, God gives us joy. God breaks us down so he can build us up. When he does, he gives us joy at who we became. A third quality Christ's righteousness produces in us is peace.

Christ's Righteousness Produces Peace in Us

When the Holy Spirit gave us Christ's righteousness, it also produced peace within us. The English word peace is based on the Hebrew word *shalom* and the Greek word *eireinei*, both of which mean "without agitation or distress due to sin." When God gave us Christ's righteousness, we were righteous. God then saved us out of the sinful world and placed us into his kingdom. Being members of his kingdom, God no longer dispensed his wrath against us, and we have peace. Isaiah 32:17 says, "The effect of righteousness will be peace."

In our naturally sinful states, we were part of the sinful world, and God's wrath was against us. We were not righteous, and God did not give us peace. Because of our sin, God made us constantly agitated and anxious. Romans 1:18 says, "For the wrath of God is revealed from heaven against all ungodliness and unrighteousness of men." God revealed his wrath by causing us to experience discomfort and pain because of our sin. We knew we were sinning because we experienced God's wrath in different ways based on the kind and degree of our sin. On our own, there was nothing we could do to get the peace of God. There was no amount of praying or self-affliction that we could have done to get God to give us his peace or to make peace with him.

However, when the Holy Spirit made us righteous, he gave us God's peace. God's peace is not like the peace we have when we are alone in a mountain cabin with no distractions as this kind of peace is synonymous with quietness. The peace of God is a state of our not receiving distress or agitation from God because of our sin. Because God gave us his peace, we are like the woman in Luke 7:50 whom Jesus healed. He told her, "Your faith has saved you; go in peace." Because of Christ's work, God tells us the same thing. A fourth quality Christ's righteousness produces in us is patience.

Christ's Righteousness Produces Patience in Us

When the Holy Spirit gave us Christ's righteousness, it produced patience within us. The English word patience is from the Hebrew word *arek* and the Greek word *makrothumia*, both of which mean "willing to endure suffering."[81] God gives us the quality of patience and makes us willing to suffer pain or hardship because of our righteousness. It is inevitable that we as Christians will be mistreated and misspoken to. We are righteous and part of a kingdom that will remain. The unrighteous outside the kingdom will be destroyed. This causes a tension between non-Christians and us. However, the Holy Spirit gave us the willingness to suffer discomfort for being righteous. Sometimes people may assume patience is the willingness to have to wait for something without complaining such as when a person must wait in line. This is only one minor aspect of patience. The concept of biblical patience is much broader. It pertains to our willingness to endure any kind of hardship, pain, or discomfort for being righteous and part of the kingdom.

In our naturally sinful states, we did not have patience. When we experienced pain or discomfort in some way, we attempted to mitigate or remove it. We did not want to be mistreated or have someone take something that belonged to us. If someone took money from us, it caused us discomfort. We attempted to remove the discomfort by trying to get it back.

However, when the Holy Spirit made us righteous, he gave us patience. We as Christians can exercise patience in numerous areas of our lives. If we are made fun of because of our righteousness, we can exercise patience and not make fun of someone in return. Even if we are persecuted, we can exercise patience and not fight back. A

---

[81] The word *patience* is related to the word *patient* who is a person enduring or tolerating an ailment.

prominent passage that deals with patience is 2 Timothy 2. In this passage the Apostle Paul is teaching Pastor Timothy about how he should act around non-Christians as he ministers. Paul tells him in 2:24, "And the Lord's servant must not be quarrelsome but kind to everyone…patiently enduring evil." Paul told Timothy that when he was ministering, and a non-Christian mistreated him or misspoke to him, he should not do the same back. Timothy had to be willing to accept the discomfort or pain for being righteous. A fifth quality Christ's righteousness produces in us is kindness.

Christ's Righteousness Produces Kindness in Us

When the Holy Spirit gave us Christ's righteousness, it produced kindness in us. Kindness is the noun version of the adjective kind. When we are kind, we are inclined to help or provide something needed to another person without expecting anything in return. The English word kindness is based on the Hebrew word *chesed* and the Greek word *chrestoteis* both of which refer to acts of kindness either by God or people. Because we have kindness, we desire to help others in different ways such as showing hospitality, giving material items, or providing consolation. When we do, we intentionally provide it, and expect nothing in return. We see an example of kindness in 2 Samuel 9 when David desired to show kindness to Mephibosheth. 2 Samuel 9:7 says, "I will show you kindness [chesed] for the sake of your father Jonathan, and I will restore to you all the land of Saul your father, and you shall eat at my table always." David showed kindness to Mephibosheth by restoring land and providing food to him.

When we were naturally sinful and part of the sinful world, we did not have kindness. We did not help or give to others unless we could obtain something in return. If we did help or give something to someone, we kept a mental account of our acts of kindness, and expected something in return at some point. This is simply how people act who are naturally sinful and part of the sinful world. They do not naturally show kindness and give without expecting something in return.

However, when the Holy Spirit made us righteous, he gave us kindness, and we can give to others without expecting anything in return. Some of us may misunderstand the concept of kindness and think it means to be considerate or nice. These synonyms do not convey the clear meaning of the word. To be kind is to help and provide things to another person so his welfare is upheld without expecting him to do the same with us. This is why the word kind is related to the word kin or kindred. Our kin are our relatives or family members. We usually give to and share with our family members the things they need. When we give to and share with someone outside our family, we are being kind because we are doing to outsiders what we do to our family or kin. A sixth quality Christ's righteousness produces in us is goodness.

Christ's Righteousness Produces Goodness in Us

When the Holy Spirit gave us Christ's righteousness, it produced goodness in us. The English word good is based on the Hebrew word *tube* and the Greek words *agathosune* and *kalos*, all of which mean "being in a state of high quality." If we have goodness or we are good, we are in a state of high quality for a specific purpose. Something or someone can have goodness and be good in different ways. For example, an object such as a painting can be good in the sense of being beautiful in an earthly way. Something such as a person can be good in the sense of being morally upright. An object or a person can be good in different ways, but in each way they are in a state of high quality.

One verse in the Scriptures that brings out this meaning is Genesis 2:9 because it uses the word good in two different ways. It says, "And out of the ground the Lord God made to spring up every tree that is pleasant to the sight and good for food. The tree of life was in the midst of the garden, and the tree of the knowledge of good and evil." The first occurrence of the word good in this verse pertains to the tree being in a state of high earthly quality. The second occurrence pertains to the tree being in a state of high spiritual quality. In both uses, the word good is used to convey the meaning of a state of high quality.

When we were in our naturally sinful states and part of the sinful world, we did not have goodness. We were not good, and we were not in a position where we could glorify God. We may have tried to be good and do what was right, but we could only mimic Christians. Even then, we only did what was right in order to acquire something for ourselves as that is the reason non-Christians do what is right. A non-Christian follows traffic laws or tax laws in order to keep from getting in trouble. He only does what is right to keep from getting in trouble, not because he has goodness within him.

However, when the Holy Spirit gave us Christ's righteousness, he made us good. We do what is right, moral, and glorifying to God because we are of high spiritual quality. We see that this is true when we enter sinful types of environments. For example, some Christians work secular jobs. Most companies have a subculture of sin. There are often numerous things that the employees of the company do that are sinful. They show up late, they call in sick when they are not, and they steal property from the company, etc. The employees do these sins because the company tolerates them as a means of maintaining morale or unity. However, Christians who work for the company do not do them because they are inherently good. Their engaging in these sins goes against who they are. A seventh quality Christ's righteousness produces in us is goodness.

Christ's Righteousness Produces Faithfulness in Us

When the Holy Spirit gave us Christ's righteousness, it produced faithfulness in us. Faithfulness is the noun version of the adjective faithful. Faithfulness is based on the Hebrew word *emunah* and Greek word *pistis*, both of which mean "the quality of being loyalty to someone." Faithfulness and loyalty are synonyms and have the same meaning. The Scriptures use faithfulness much more than loyalty, though. In the Scriptures, the Holy Spirit uses the concept of faithfulness to describe a husband or wife's loyalty to the other or a servant's loyalty to his master. More prominently, however, the Holy Spirit uses faithfulness to describe God's loyalty to his people and his promises to them. 2 Timothy 2:13 says, "If we are faithless, he remains faithful."

When we were naturally sinful in the sinful world, we did not have faithfulness. We only had loyalty to ourselves. We could rely on ourselves to please ourselves, but God could not trust us to live for his glory. We see this repeatedly with Israel in the Old Testament. They constantly turned from God to other gods even when God blessed them. God could not trust most of them to be loyal to him. We were the same in our naturally sinful states. We had no loyalty to anyone, but to ourselves.

We can understand the concept of loyalty or faithfulness by looking at organized crime. One of the more prominent characteristics about men who have been involved in organized crime is that they were loyal to their bosses, at least most of the time. They had to be loyal because getting a job in organized crime did not usually involve a job application and a W-4 form. Loyalty held the crime boss and his associates together when there was no paperwork. However, their loyalty was earthly in nature, and their loyalty could disappear under the right circumstances. This kind of loyalty is not the kind of loyalty that God gives us. When the Holy Spirit made us righteous and placed us into the kingdom, he gave us the quality of faithfulness. We are faithful or loyal to God as his subjects within his kingdom and live to glorify him. An eighth quality Christ's righteousness produces in us is gentleness.

Christ's Righteousness Produces Gentleness in Us

When the Holy Spirit gave us Christ's righteousness, it produced gentleness in us. The word gentleness is the quality of not being violent, harsh, or forceful toward others.

The English word gentle is based on the Hebrew words *anavah* and *rak* and the Greek word *prauteis*, all of which have this meaning. Because we have gentleness, we do not use force to get our way. Even if we do not like the way things are or how we are affected by the way things are, we do not coerce or intimidate people in order to change things so we are satisfied.

We may think that our being gentle means we are weak or soft. If we think this, we are confusing two issues. One pertains to how we treat others and the other pertains to how we handle being treated by others. When we treat others without using force or intimidation to get our way we are gentle. Moreover, when others mistreat us, but we maintain our composure, we are patient or tough. So, on the one hand, we should be gentle in how we treat others, but on the other hand, we should be patient or tough when we are mistreated by others. This principle is often communicated through the modern-day proverb, "Have thick skin (toughness or patience), but a soft heart (gentleness)."

A prime example of this principle is Jesus himself. Jesus was gentle toward others and spoke words without being violent or harsh toward them. He did not impose his will on others, and did not coerce anyone to obey God or turn from sin. Jesus was also patient. People mistreated him both verbally and physically. He allowed it without complaining or losing his composure. People mistreated him in many ways, and eventually put him to death without his even saying a word to prevent it or get revenge. Jesus was a paragon of gentleness as well as patience.

When we were naturally sinful and part of the sinful world, we did not have gentleness. We used force or coercion in different ways in order to get something we wanted or to have our interests met. Sometimes we used physical force such when we used our car to prevent another car from moving somewhere on the road. Other times, we used various forms of verbal manipulation, intimidation, or coercion such as when we told someone something in order to get them to do what we wanted. As naturally sinful people, we did not have gentleness.

However, when the Holy Spirit made us righteous, he gave us the quality of gentleness. We have the quality that enables us to refrain from using force or violence to get our way and have our interests met. We may explain what our desires are, and give reasons for them, but we do use any kind of violence or force to have them met. This is why Proverbs 15:1 says, "A gentle answer turns away wrath, but a harsh word stirs up anger." Even when we must deal with people who impose their will on us, we can refrain from being harsh or forceful with them. A ninth quality Christ's righteousness produces in us is self-control.

Christ's Righteousness Produces Self-control in Us

When the Holy Spirit gave us Christ's righteousness, it produced self-control in us. Self-control is the discipline within us that allows us to restrain from engaging in sin. The English word self-control is based on the Hebrew phrase, *mosheal beruaho*, which means "rules over his spirit." It is also based on the Greek word *egkrateia*, which means "inner strength." Though this Hebrew phrase and Greek word are only used a few times in the Scriptures, the principle occurs throughout them. When the Holy Spirit gave us Christ's righteousness, we still had a body that was naturally sinful. Our righteous spirits wanted to please God, but our sinful bodies wanted to sin. However, part of having Christ's righteousness involved having the quality of self-control so we can overcome the sin within our bodies and obey God. As the Holy Spirit teaches us, we can exercise self-control and do what is right. Galatians 5:16 says, "Walk by [with] the Spirit, and you will not gratify the desires of the flesh."

Before the Holy Spirit gave us Christ's righteousness, we did not have self-control. We may have had a level of discipline that allowed us to refrain from certain sins at certain times under certain conditions. However, we did not have the self-control to refrain from engaging in any sin under any condition at any time. Given certain circumstances and pressures, we would have sinned, and we did. As we think about it, it makes sense. Anytime we sin, we are literally out of control; i.e. out of self-control. We sinned because we could not control ourselves.

However, when the Holy Spirit gave us Christ's righteousness, we acquired self-control. There is one notable instance in Scriptures in which the principle of self-control is dealt with. In 1 Corinthians 7, there were some Christians in the Corinthian church who lacked self-control in the area of sexual temptation. The Holy Spirit knew they lacked self-control in this area. It may have been because they lived in a culture of sexual promiscuity or they may have had a background where they engaged in immoral sexual activities. We do not know for sure, but the Spirit did. He also knew that when one spouse deprived the other of sexual intimacy, the other was tempted to seek intimacy outside of the marriage. So, the Spirit said to them as well as to us in 1 Corinthians 7:5, "Do not deprive one another…but then come together again, so that Satan may not tempt you because of your lack of self-control."

Christ's Righteousness Includes Other Fruit

Christ's righteousness produces these nine qualities in us. The Spirit refers to these qualities as his "fruit" because he produces them in us when he gives us Christ's righteousness. These nine character traits, however, are not the only ones. Christ's righteousness will produce other qualities in us as well such as gratitude, mercifulness, and confidence. We know this because the Holy Spirit says in Galatians 5:21, "and things like these" in reference to the deeds of the flesh. Through inference, we also apply this phrase to the fruit of the Spirit. We consider these nine qualities as examples of the qualities that Christ's righteousness will produce in us. Christ's righteousness produces within each of us every quality that God wants us to have so we glorify him.

Trials Develop Christ's Righteousness and Form Our Character

As Christians, we all have experienced trials of some kind. When we did, we may not have connected them to God's work in us. Though it may not be acceptable to some of us, God causes us to experience trials as a means to develop his qualities in us. We have God's qualities, but we also have sin within our body. As we experience trials and various types of sufferings, they give us a taste of God's wrath. In response, we turn away from sin, and strive to live in accordance with Christ's righteousness with us. After the trial has passed, we are less sinful and display God's qualities more than we did before the trail. The ratio of these qualities within us to the sin within us is our character. Because of this, Romans 5:4 says, "Suffering produces endurance, and endurance produces character." Christ's righteousness produces fruit within us, and the ratio between our fruit and our sin is our character.

We can see the concept God's imposing trials on us to build our character through the analogy of metallurgy. In metallurgy, a smith obtains a certain kind of metal such as gold. If he obtains the gold directly from the ground, it may contain impurities. The smith removes the impurities by putting the gold in a furnace. The intense heat of the furnace causes the impurities to separate from the raw gold. After the gold goes through the furnace, it is much purer than it was before. Proverbs 27:21 says, "The crucible is for silver, and the furnace is for gold." In the same way, God causes us to experience trials so we will turn from our sin, and display godly character more than we did before the trial.

Christ's Righteousness Causes Us to Glorify God

A counselor was speaking with a new patient one day and was trying to get to know him. As they were speaking, the counselor asked the patient who he was. The patient told the counselor his name, where he was from, and what he did for a living. The counselor then explained to his patient that those things did not pertain to who he was. When the counselor asked the patient who he was, he wanted to know about the patient's character. Our character is the level of Christ's righteousness we display in our lives. A person of strong character displays more of Christ's righteousness than a person of weak character.

As we live with Christ's righteousness, the qualities it produces automatically show up in our thoughts, words, and actions. We cannot break the link between who we are and how we live. Matthew 7:17 and 20 says, "So, every healthy tree bears good fruit, but the diseased tree bears bad fruit. Thus you will recognize them by their fruits." We as Christians live with God's qualities because they are part of who we are. We as Christians have different names, we live in different places, and we have different jobs on this earth, but we are not identified by these things. Our identity is with Christ so that we have his righteousness within us, and we are part of his righteous kingdom. Galatians 2:20 says, "I have been crucified with Christ. It is no longer I who live, but Christ who lives in me." God specifically saved us to live in his righteous kingdom. He specifically saved us to display the qualities that Christ's righteousness produces in us. No one can change this about us. When we display Christ's righteousness in our lives, then and only then can we glorify God and fulfill the purpose for which he made us.

Conclusion

We have learned about the details of our salvation. We have discovered all the work God did to make us righteous, save us out of this sinful world, and bring us into his kingdom. Of everything God did, however, we cannot change any of it. We may have read things that we disagreed with or things that may not have been to our liking. However, we cannot negotiate with God to have them changed. God saved us by working in a very specific way to accomplish a specific purpose.

Before anything existed, God existed. He was full of glory, magnificence, and splendor which no words from our mouths could appropriately describe. God then began to work in such a perfect and incomprehensible way. The volumes of scientific literature describing God's creation can by no means begin to articulate his work. When God spoke the creation into existence, every moment of time which elapsed and every indiscernible movement through space resulted in a people who would ultimately display his very qualities and reflect his glory in his kingdom.

God's kingdom is ubiquitous across the earth. It began with Christ himself and continued to grow without restriction across national boundaries, language barriers, and cultural norms. Nothing can stop God from building it, and nothing can prevent God from placing a person in it. It would be easier for us to stop the earth from rotating than it would be to stop God from building his kingdom of people. It would be easier for us to stop the earth from rotating than it would be to stop God from building his kingdom of people. God is building his kingdom with people who have lived in various places and at various times in history. We think about the soldiers sitting on the battlefield during the Greco-Persian War hundreds of years ago. We think about the people currently selling food in the rural areas of the northern Philippines. We think about the people who will live years from now whose parents have not yet even been born. Throughout all of history and across the entire earth, God has been building and will continue to build his kingdom with people such as these. These people were not worthy on their own and did nothing to earn a place within God's kingdom. God chose to create them long before time began and place them into his kingdom so they would glorify him.

Every one of us entered God's kingdom like a child longing for his true home. The kingdom is where we belong. Someone could threaten us with death, but even death could not coerce us to give up the kingdom. Someone could offer us the riches of the earth to follow the sinfulness of the present age, but even these could not dissuade us from living in the kingdom and obeying our king. God saved out of the sinful world and placed us into his kingdom so we would glorify him. This is who we are and why we exist.

Michael Jones is available for interviews and personal appearances. For more information or requests email the publisher at: info@advbooks.com

To purchase additional copies of this book, visit our bookstore website at: www.advbookstore.com

"we bring dreams to life" ™
www.advbookstore.com

www.ingramcontent.com/pod-product-compliance
Lightning Source LLC
Chambersburg PA
CBHW062216080426
42734CB00010B/1911